Daily Help

Daily Help

Charles Spurgeon

Whitaker House

All Scripture quotations are from the *King James Version* (KJV) of
the Bible.

DAILY HELP

ISBN: 0-88368-407-1
Printed in the United States of America
Copyright © 1996 by Whitaker House

Whitaker House
580 Pittsburgh Street
Springdale, PA 15144

2 3 4 5 6 7 8 9 10 11 / 06 05 04 03 02 01 00 99 98 97 96

January 1

*W*e will be glad and rejoice in You. We will not open the gates of the year to the mournful notes of the trombone but to the sweet strains of the harp of joy. "O come, let us sing unto the LORD: let us make a joyful noise to the rock of our salvation" (Ps. 95:1). What heavens are laid up in Jesus! What rivers of infinite bliss have their source and every drop of their fullness in Him! Since, sweet Lord Jesus, You are the present portion of Your people, favor us this year with such a sense of Your preciousness that from its first to its last day, we may be glad and rejoice in You.

January 2

*H*e who lives without prayer, he who lives with little prayer, he who seldom reads the Word, and he who seldom looks up to heaven for a fresh influence from on high—he will be the man whose heart will become dry and barren. However, he who falls in secret on his God, who spends much time in holy retirement, who delights to meditate on the words of the Most High, and whose soul is given up to Christ—such a man must have an overflowing heart. As his heart is, such will his life be.

January 3

*A*ll my springs are in thee" (Ps. 87:7), and if you have all your springs in God, your heart will be full enough. If you go to the foot of Calvary, there your heart will be bathed in love and gratitude. If you frequent the vale of retirement, and there talk with your God, it is there that your heart will be full of calm resolve. If you go out with your Master to the hill of Olivet and look down with Him upon a wicked Jerusalem and weep over it with Him, then will your heart be full of love for never-dying souls.

January 4

*D*o not keep back part of the price. (See Acts 5:3.) Make a full surrender of every motion of your heart. Labor to have but one object and one aim, and for this purpose give God the keeping of your heart. Cry out for more of the divine influences of the Holy Spirit so that when your soul is preserved and protected by Him it may be directed into one channel and one only. Then your life may run deep and pure and clear and peaceful, its only banks being God's will, its only channel the love of Christ and a desire to please Him.

January 5

*N*ever, never neglect the word of God that will make your heart rich with precept and with understanding. Then your conversation, when it flows from your mouth, will be like your heart: rich, savory, and spiritually fervent. Make your heart full of rich, generous love, and then the stream that flows from your hand will be just as rich and generous as your heart. Oh, go, Christian, to the great mine of riches, and cry unto the Holy Spirit to make your heart rich unto salvation. Then will your life and conversation be a blessing to your fellows, and when they see you, your face will be as the angel of God.

January 6

*T*here is not a spider hanging on the king's wall that does not have its errand; there is not a nettle that grows in the corner of the churchyard that does not have its purpose; there is not a single insect fluttering in the breeze that does not accomplish some divine decree; and I will never have it that God created any man, especially any Christian man, to be a blank and to be a nothing. He made you for an end. Find out what that end is. Find out your niche and fill it. If it is ever so little, if it is only to be a chopper of wood and a drawer of water, do something in this great battle for God and truth.

January 7

Suppose you see a lake, and there are twenty or thirty streams running into it. Why, there will not be one strong river in the whole country; there will be a number of little brooks which will be dried up in the summer and will be temporary torrents in winter. Every one of them will be useless for any great purpose because there is not enough water in the lake to feed more than one great stream. Now, a man's heart has only enough life in it to pursue one object fully. You must not give half your love to Christ and the other half to the world. "No man can serve two masters...Ye cannot serve God and mammon" (Matt. 6:24).

January 8

Prayer is the rustling of the wings of the angels that are on their way bringing us the blessings of heaven. Have you heard prayer in your heart? You will see the angel in your house. When the chariots that bring us blessings do rumble, their wheels do sound with prayer. We hear the prayer in our own spirits, and that prayer becomes the token of the coming blessings. Even as the cloud foreshadows rain, so prayer foreshadows the blessing; even as the green blade is the beginning of the harvest, so prayer is the prophecy of the blessing that is about to come.

January 9

Omnipotence may build a thousand worlds and fill them with bounties. Omnipotence may powder mountains into dust and burn the sea and consume the sky, but Omnipotence cannot do an unloving thing toward a believer. Oh, rest quite sure, Christian, a hard thing, an unloving thing, from God toward one of His own people is quite impossible. He is as kind to you when He casts you into prison as when He takes you into a palace; He is as good when He sends famine into your house as when He fills your barns with plenty. The only question is, Are you His child? If so, He has rebuked you in affection, and there is love in His chastisement.

January 10

Do you not know that God is an eternal, self-existent Being, that to say He loves now is, in fact, to say He always did love since with God there is no past and can be no future. What we call past, present, and future, He wraps in one eternal now. And if you say He loves you now, you say He loved yesterday, He loved in the past eternity, and He will love forever, for now with God is past, present, and future.

Christ's love is the sun, and our love is the moonlight which we are able to give forth because of the sun's light upon us.

January 11

*I*f any one should ask me for an abstract of the Christian religion, I should say it is in that one word *prayer*. If I should be asked, "What will take in the whole of Christian experience?" I should answer, "prayer." A man must have been convinced of sin before he could pray; he must have had some hope that there was mercy for him before he could pray. All the Christian virtues are locked up in the word *prayer*.

In troubling times our best communion with God will be carried on by supplication. Tell Him your case, search out His promise, and then plead it with holy boldness. This is the best, the surest, and the speediest way of relief.

January 12

*S*inner, let this be your comfort, that God sees you when you begin to repent. He does not see you with His usual gaze with which He looks on all men, but He sees you with an eye of intense interest. He has been looking on you in all your sin and in all your sorrow, hoping that you would repent, and now He sees the first gleam of grace and beholds it with joy. Never did a watchman on the lonely castle top see the first gray light of morning with more joy than that with which God beholds the first desire in your heart.

January 13

*A*s sure as God is God, if you this day are seeking Him aright, through Christ, the day will come when the kiss of full assurance will be on your lips, when the arms of sovereign love will embrace you, and you will know it to be so. You may have despised Him, but you will know Him yet to be your Father and your Friend. You may have broken His Sabbaths and despised His Word; the day is coming when the Sabbath will be your delight and His Word your treasure.

January 14

*T*he great King, immortal, invisible, the Divine Person, called the Holy Ghost, the Holy Spirit—it is He that quickens the soul, or else it would lie dead forever. It is He that makes it tender, or else it would never feel. It is He that imparts efficacy to the Word preached, or else it could never reach further than the ear. It is He who breaks the heart; it is He who makes it whole.

There dwells upon this earth a mysterious Being whose office is to renew the fallen and restore the wandering. We cannot see Him or hear Him, yet He dwells in some of us as Lord of our nature. His chosen residence is "a broken heart" and "a contrite spirit" (Ps. 34:18).

*D*elight in divine service is a token of acceptance. Those who serve God with a sad countenance, because they do what is unpleasant to them, are not serving Him at all; they bring the form of homage, but the life is absent. That obedience which is not voluntary is disobedience, for the Lord looks at the heart. If He sees that we serve Him from force, and not because we love Him, He will reject our offering. Service coupled with cheerfulness is heart-service and, therefore, true. Take away joyful willingness from the Christian, and you have removed the test of his sincerity.

Cheerfulness is the support of our strength; in the joy of the Lord we are strong. (See Nehemiah 8:10.)

January 16

*T*he river of God is full of water, but there is not one drop of it that takes its rise in earthly springs. God will have no strength used in His own battles but the strength which He himself imparts, and I would not have you that are now distressed discouraged by it. Your emptiness is but the preparation for your being filled, and your casting down is but the making ready for your lifting up.

Unexpected help will come to us when affairs are at their worst.

Let us learn from our Master to reckon upon forces invisible.

I gaze on beauty and may be myself deformed. I admire the light and may yet dwell in darkness, but if the light of the countenance of God rests upon me, I will become like Him. The countenance of His visage will be on me, and the great outlines of His attributes will be mine. Oh, wondrous glass, which renders the beholder lovely. Oh, admirable mirror, which reflects not self with its imperfections but gives a perfect image to those that are not comely.

If you do continually draw your impulse, your life, the whole of your being from the Holy Spirit, then you will see God and Jesus face to face.

January 18

N othing gives the believer so much joy as fellowship with Christ. He has enjoyment as others have in the common mercies of life. He can be glad both in God's gifts and God's works, but in all these separately and in all of them added together, he does not find such substantial delight as in the matchless person of his Lord Jesus.

Where can such sweetness be found as we have tasted in communion with our Beloved?

If you know anything of the inner life, you will confess that our highest, purest, and most enduring joys must be the fruit of the "tree of life, which is in the midst of the paradise of God" (Rev. 2:7).

January 19

*H*ow encouraging is the thought of the Redeemer's never-ceasing intercession for us. When we pray, He pleads for us, and when we are not praying, He is advocating our cause and, by His supplications, shielding us from unseen dangers. We little know what we owe to our Savior's prayers. When we reach the hilltops of heaven and look back upon all the way whereby the Lord our God has led us, how we will praise Him who, before the eternal throne, has pleaded our cause against our unseen enemies. "But I have prayed for thee, that thy faith fail not" (Luke 22:32).

January 20

*J*esus answered and said, I thank thee, O Father" (Matt. 11:25). It was the habit and life of Jesus to talk with God. May we likewise have silent fellowship with the Father so that we may answer Him often. Though the world knows not to whom we speak, may we be responding to that secret voice, unheard of by any other ear, which our own ear, opened by the Spirit of God, recognizes with joy. What a privilege is intimate communion with the Father of our spirits! It is a secret hidden from the world, a joy with which even the nearest friend cannot interfere.

This very day may our hearts be in such a state that when God speaks to us, we, like Jesus, may be prepared at once to answer Him.

January 21

*B*eloved, while we do not neglect external things, which are good enough in themselves, we ought also to see to it that we enjoy living, personal fellowship with Jesus. See to it that sitting at the Savior's feet is not neglected, even though it is under the specious pretext of doing Him service. The first thing for our soul's health, the first thing for His glory, and the first thing for our own usefulness is to keep ourselves in perpetual communion with the Lord Jesus and to see that the vital spirituality of our religion is maintained over and above everything else in the world.

January 22

*B*oldly come unto the King of Kings from whom no sincere petitioner ever was dismissed unheard.

Whenever there is a heart big with sorrow, wherever there is an eye suffused with tears, wherever there is a lip quivering with agony, wherever there is a deep groan or a penitential sigh, the ear of Jehovah is wide open. He puts our prayers, like rose leaves, between the pages of His book of remembrance, and when the volume is opened at last, there will be a precious fragrance springing up from there.

January 23

*I*t is well to be the sheep of God's pasture, even if we have been wandering sheep. The straying sheep has an owner, and however far it may stray from the fold, it does not cease to belong to that owner. I believe that God will yet bring back into the fold every one of His own sheep, and they will all be saved. It is something to feel our wanderings, for if we feel ourselves to be lost, we will certainly be saved. If we feel ourselves to have wandered, we will certainly be brought back.

January 24

*I*f you might go to heaven and hold communion with some person whom you dearly loved, you would often be found there. But here is Jesus, the King of heaven, and He gives you that which can open the gates of heaven and let you in to be with Him. Yet, you live without meditating upon His work, meditating upon His person, meditating upon His offices, and meditating upon His glory. Ah, there is nothing that can so console your spirits and relieve all your distresses and troubles as the feeling that now you can meditate on the person of Jesus Christ.

January 25

*I*n the very beginning, when this great universe lay in the mind of God like unborn forests in the acorn-cup, long before the echoes walked the solitudes, before the mountains were brought forth, and long before the light flashed through the sky, God loved His chosen creatures. Before there was creatureship—when the ether was not fanned by the angel's wing, when space itself had not an existence, when there was nothing save God alone—even then, in that loneliness of Deity and in that deep quiet and profundity, His love moved for His chosen. Their names were written on His heart, and they were then dear to His soul.

January 26

*G*od is love in its highest degree. He is love rendered more than love. Love is not God, but God is love. He is full of grace; He is the plenitude of mercy; He "delighteth in mercy" (Mic. 7:18).

I believe that every flower in a garden which is tended by a wise gardener could tell of some particular care that the gardener takes of it. He does for the dahlia what he does not for the sunflower; something is wanted by the rose that is not required by the lily; and the geranium calls for an attention which is not given to the honeysuckle. Each flower wins from the gardener a special culture.

He loves us better than we love ourselves.

January 27

*F*riendship with God the Father is most needed in order to be happy in the life to come, and happiness in this life is dependent on friends. True friendship can only be made between true men. Hearts are the soul of honor. There can be no lasting friendship between bad men. Bad men may pretend to love each other, but their friendship is a rope of sand which will be broken at any convenient season. However, if a man has a sincere heart within him, and is true and noble, then we may confide in him.

January 28

*T*he imagination will sometimes fly up to God with such a power that eagles' wings cannot match it. It sometimes has such might that it can almost see the King in His beauty and the land which is very far off. But if it is potent one way, it is also another, for imagination has taken us down to the lowest plains of earth. But I rejoice and think of one thing, that I can cry out when this imagination comes upon me. So it is with the Christian. If he cries out, there is hope. Can you chain your imagination? No, but the power of the Holy Spirit can. Ah, this power will do it! And it does do it at last; it does it even on earth.

*T*he hour is coming, and it may be even now, when the Holy Spirit will be poured out again in such a wonderful manner that "many shall run to and fro, and knowledge shall be increased" (Dan. 12:4). The knowledge of the Lord will cover the earth as the waters cover the surface of the great deep (Isa. 11:9). The hour is coming when His kingdom will come and His will shall be done on earth even as it is in heaven (Matt. 6:10) and when every one will see that truly the Spirit is poured out like water and the rains are descending from above. For that let us pray; let us continually labor for it and seek it of God.

*G*od's Holy Spirit and man's sin cannot live together peaceably. They may both be in the same heart, but they cannot both reign there. Nor can they both be quiet there, for "the flesh lusteth against the Spirit, and the Spirit against the flesh" (Gal. 5:17). They cannot rest, but there will be a perpetual warring in the soul so that the Christian will have to cry, "O wretched man that I am! who shall deliver me from the body of this death?" (Rom. 7:24). But in due time, the Spirit will drive out all sin and will present us blameless before the throne of His Majesty with exceedingly great joy.

Simeon called Jesus "the consolation of Israel" (Luke 2:25), and so He was. Before His actual appearance, His name was the Day-Star—cheering the darkness and prophet of the rising sun. To Him they looked with the same hope which cheers the nightly watcher when from the lonely castle top he sees the fairest of the stars and hails her as the usher of the morn. When He was on earth, He must have been the consolation of all those who were privileged to be His companions. Like children, they would tell Him of their grief and consider Him as the Father.

February 1

*O*h, it must have been sweet to have lived with Christ. Surely, sorrows were then only joys in masks because they gave one an opportunity to go to Jesus to have them removed. Oh, would to God, some of us may say that we could have laid our weary heads upon the bosom of Jesus and that our birth had been in that happy era when we might have heard His kind voice when he said, "Let the weary ones come unto me." (See Matthew 11:28.) But hear how kindly Jesus speaks: "I will not leave you comfortless...I will pray the Father, and he shall give you another Comforter, that he may abide with you for ever" (John 14:18, 16).

February 2

*O*ur world has two forces. It has one tendency to run off at a tangent from its orbit, but the sun draws it by a centripetal power and attracts it to itself. Oh, Christian, you will never walk aright and keep in the orbit of truth if it is not for the influence of Christ perpetually attracting you to the center. Christ is drawing you to Himself, to His likeness, to His character, to His love, and to His bosom; and in that way you are kept from your natural tendency to fly off and be lost in the wide fields of sin. Bless God that Christ lifted up draws all His people to Him. (See John 12:32.)

February 3

*I*t is better to have two lights than only one. The light of creation is a bright light. God may be seen in the stars; His name is written in gilt letters on the brow of night. You may discover His glory in the ocean waves or in the trees of the field, but it is better to read it in two books than in one. You will find it here in the Holy Scriptures more clearly revealed, for He has written this book Himself, and He has given you the key to understand it if you have the Holy Spirit. Ah, beloved, let us thank God for this Bible; let us love it; and let us count it more precious "than much fine gold" (Ps. 19:10).

February 4

*I*f we had the blessings without asking for them, we should think them common things, but prayer makes the common pebbles of God's temporal bounties more precious than diamonds. Spiritual prayer cuts the diamond and makes it glisten more.

When you are wrestling like Jacob with the angel and are nearly thrown down, ask the Holy Spirit to strengthen your arm. Consider how the Holy Spirit is the chariot-wheel of prayer. Prayer may be the chariot, the desire may draw it forth, but the Spirit is the very wheel whereby it moves.

February 5

*T*here are moments when the eyes glisten with joy, and we can say, "we are persuaded, confident, certain." I do not wish to distress anyone who is under doubt. Often gloomy doubts will prevail. There are seasons when you fear you have not been called, when you doubt your interest in Christ. Ah, what a mercy it is that it is not your hold of Christ that saves you but His hold of you! What a sweet fact that it is not how you grasp His hand but His grasp of yours that saves you.

The Lord's promise, once given, is never taken back.

February 6

*T*he Gospel is the sum of wisdom, an epitome of knowledge, a treasure house of truth, and a revelation of mysterious secrets. Our meditation upon it enlarges the mind, and as it opens to our soul in successive flashes of glory, we stand astonished at the profound wisdom manifest in it. Ah, dear friends, if you seek wisdom, you will see it displayed in all its greatness. But turn aside and see this great sight—an incarnate God upon the cross, a substitute atoning for mortal guilt, and a sacrifice satisfying the vengeance of heaven and delivering the rebellious sinner. Here is essential wisdom enthroned, crowned, and glorified.

February 7

*D*o you know, saint, how much the Holy Spirit loves you? Can you measure the love of the Spirit? Do you know how great is the affection of His soul towards you? Go measure heaven with your span; go weigh the mountains in the scales; go take the ocean's water and calculate each drop; go count the sand upon the sea's wide shore; and when you have accomplished this, you can tell how much He loves you. He has loved you long; He has loved you well; He loved you ever; and He still will love you. Surely, He is the person to comfort you because He loves.

February 8

*S*ome people say they cannot bear to be an hour in solitude; they have got nothing to do, nothing to think about. No Christian will ever talk so, surely, for I can but give him one word to think of, Christ. Let him spell that over forever. Let me give him the word, Jesus. Only let him try to think it over, and he will find that an hour is nothing and that eternity is not half enough to utter our glorious Savior's praise.

From a sweet fountain of thought we will have sweet waters of talk. It is sweet to live in the thoughts of those we love.

February 9

*T*he canon revelation is closed; there is no more to be added. God does not give a fresh revelation, but He rivets the old one. When it has been forgotten and laid in the dusty chamber of our memories, He brings it forth and cleans the picture but does not paint a new one. It is not by any new revelation that the Spirit comforts. He does so by telling us old things over again. He brings a fresh lamp to manifest the treasures hidden in Scripture. He unlocks the strong chests in which the truth has long lain, and He points to secret chambers filled with untold riches but coins no more because enough is done.

February 10

*M*ost of the grand truths of God have to be learned by trouble. They must be burned into us with the hot iron of affliction; otherwise, we will not truly receive them. No man is competent to judge in matters of the kingdom until he has first been tried, since there are many things to be learned in the depths which we can never know in the heights. He who has had wants himself will best meet those wants of God's people. He who has needed comfort will best comfort God's Israel. He who has felt his own need of salvation will best preach it.

February 11

*I*f I desired to put myself in the most likely place for the Lord to meet with me, I should prefer the house of prayer, for it is in preaching that the Word is most blessed. Still, I think I should equally desire the reading of the Scriptures, for I might pause over every verse and say, "Such a verse was blessed to so many souls, then, why not to me? I am at least in the pool of Bethesda. I am walking among its porches, and who can tell but that the angel will stir the pool of the Word while I lie helplessly by the side of it waiting for the blessing?"

February 12

*O*h! It is a happy way of smoothing sorrow when we can say, "We will wait only upon God." Oh, you agitated Christians, do not dishonor your religion by always wearing a brow of care. Come, cast your burden up on the Lord. I see you staggering beneath a weight which He would not feel. What seems to you a crushing burden would be to Him but as the small dust of the balance. See, the Almighty bends His shoulders, and He says, "Here, put your troubles here."

"Come unto me...and I will give you rest" (Matt. 11:28).

February 13

Christ is the chariot in which souls are drawn to heaven. The people of the Lord are on their way to heaven. They are carried in everlasting arms, and those arms are the arms of Christ. Christ is carrying them up to His own house, to His own throne. By and by His prayer, "Father, I will that they also, whom thou hast given me, be with me where I am" (John 17:24), will be wholly fulfilled. The cross is the great covenant transport which will weather out the storms and reach its desired heaven. This is the chariot; the pillars wherewith are of gold. It is lined with the purple of the atonement of our Lord Jesus Christ.

February 14

What, is Christ your brother, and does He live in your house? Yet, you have not spoken to Him for a month? I fear there is little love between you and your brother, for you have had no conversation with Him for so long. What, is Christ the husband of His church, and has she had no fellowship with Him for all this time?

Prayer is the outcome of that sense of need which arises from the new life. A man would not pray to God if he did not feel that he had an urgent need for blessings which only the Lord can bestow.

Prayer is the autograph of the Holy Spirit upon the renewed heart.

*T*o know one's self to be foolish is to stand upon the doorstep of the temple of wisdom. To understand the wrong of any position is halfway towards amending it. To be quite sure that our self-confidence is sin and folly, and an offense towards God, is a great help towards the absolute casting of our self-confidence away and the bringing of our souls, in practice as well as in theory, to rely wholly upon the power of God's Holy Spirit.

Nobody will err about the way to God if he really resolves to follow that way. The Spirit of God will guide those whose hearts are set upon coming to God.

February 16

*Y*ou cannot, though you may think you can, preserve a moderation in sin. If you commit one sin, it is like the melting of the lower glacier upon the Alps; the others must follow in time. As certainly as you heap one stone upon the mound today, the next day you will cast another until the heap, raised stone by stone, will become a very pyramid. Set the coral insect at work; you cannot decree where it will stay its work. It will not build its rock just as high as you please. It will not stay until there will be soil upon it and until an island will be created by tiny creatures. Sin cannot be held in with bit and bridle.

*F*rom the cross of Calvary, where the bleeding hands of Jesus drop mercy, from the garden of Gethsemane, the cry comes, "Look unto me, and be ye saved, all the ends of the earth" (Isa. 45:22). From Calvary's summit, where Jesus cries, "It is finished" (John 19:30), I hear a shout, "Look, and be saved." But there comes a cry from our soul, "Nay, look to yourself!" Ah, look to yourself, and you will be lost. As long as you look to yourself, there is no hope for you. It is not a consideration of what you are but a consideration of what God is, and what Christ is, that can save you.

*I*f you know these two things, yourself a sinner and Christ a Savior, it is looking from yourself to Jesus. Oh, there are men that quite misunderstand the Gospel. They think that righteousness qualifies them to come to Christ, whereas sin is the only qualification for a man to come to Jesus. Good old Crisp says, "Righteousness keeps me from Christ: 'They that are whole have no need of the physician, but they that are sick' (Mark 2:17). Sin makes me come to Jesus, when sin is felt, and in coming to Christ, the more sin I have, the more cause I have to hope for mercy."

February 19

*A*s a man does not make himself spiritually alive, so neither can he keep himself so. He can feed on spiritual food and so preserve his spiritual strength. He can walk in the commandments of the Lord and so enjoy rest and peace, but still the inner life is dependent upon the Spirit as much for its after existence as for its first begetting. No man himself, even when converted, has any power except that which is daily, constantly, and perpetually infused into him by the Spirit.

The motivation for action to a believing man is found in the realization that God, for Christ's sake, has forgiven his iniquities.

February 20

*C*ultivate a cheerful disposition. Endeavor, as much as lies in you, always to bear a smile about with you. (See John 16:33.) Recollect that this is as much a command of God as that one which says, "Thou shalt love the Lord thy God with all thy heart" (Matt. 22:37).

Let us take the pure gold of thankfulness and the jewels of praise and make them into another crown for the head of Jesus. When it is the Lord's work in which we rejoice, we need not be afraid of being too glad.

Cheerfulness is most becoming in Christian men.

Contentment is the crown jewel of a happy life.

February 21

*Y*ou may think of a doctrine forever and get no good from it if you are not already saved. However, think of the person of Christ, and that will give you faith. Take Him everywhere, wherever you go, and try to meditate on Him in your leisure moments. Then He will reveal Himself to you and give you peace.

We should all know more, live nearer to God, and grow in grace if we were more alone. Meditation chews the cud and extracts the real nourishment from the mental food gathered elsewhere.

Read the Bible carefully, and then meditate and meditate and meditate.

February 22

*T*here is no loss in being a Christian and making God the first object. But, if you make anything else your goal, with all your running, should you run ever so well, you will fall short of the mark; or if you gain it, you will fall uncrowned, unhonored to the earth. "My soul, wait thou only upon God" (Ps. 62:5).

He that serves God in body, soul, and spirit, to the utmost of his power, finds new power given to him hour by hour, for God opens to him fresh springs.

The ideal Christian is one who has been made alive with a life which he lives for God.

February 23

*T*he book of nature is an expression of the thoughts of God. We have God's terrible thoughts in the thunder and lightning, God's loving thoughts in the sunshine and the balmy breeze, God's bounteous, prudent, careful thoughts in the waving harvest and in the ripening meadow. We have God's brilliant thoughts in the wondrous scenes which are beheld from mountaintop and valley, and we have God's most sweet and pleasant thoughts of beauty in the little flowers that blossom at our feet. "God, who giveth us richly all things to enjoy" (1 Tim. 6:17).

February 24

*I*t may be that during a sermon two men are listening to the same truth. One of them hears as attentively as the other and remembers as much of it; the other is melted to tears or moved with solemn thoughts. The one, though equally attentive, sees nothing in the sermon except, maybe, certain important truths well set forth. As for the other, his heart is broken within him, and his soul is melted.

Ask me how it is that the same truth has an effect upon this one and not upon the other— because the mysterious Spirit of the living God goes with the truth to one heart and not to the other.

February 25

*T*here are some who are like what is fabled of the swan. The ancients said that the swan never sang in his lifetime but always sang just when he died. Now, there are many of God's despondent children who seem to go all their lives under a cloud, but they get a swan's song before they die. The river of their lives comes running down, perhaps black and miry with troubles, and when it begins to touch the white foam of the sea, there comes a little glistening in its waters. So, beloved, though we may have been very much dispirited by reason of the burden of the way, when we get to the end, we will have sweet songs.

February 26

*I*t is marvelous that the men who most of all rail at faith are remarkable for credulity. Not caring to have God in their hearts, forsaking the living fountain, they have hewn out for themselves cisterns which are broken and hold no water. Oh, that we may each of us be more wise, that we may not forsake the good old path or leave the way that God has prepared for us. What wonder we should travel among thorns and briars and rend our own flesh or, worse than that, fall among dark mountains and be lost among the chasms thereof if we despise the guidance of our unerring Father.

February 27

*B*ehold Him whom you cannot behold! Lift up your eyes to heaven, and see Him who stretched the heavens like a tent to dwell in and then did weave into their tapestry, with golden needle, stars that glitter in the darkness. Mark Him who spread the earth and created man upon it. He is all-sufficient, eternal, self-existent, unchangeable! Will you not reverence Him? He is good; He is loving; He is kind; He is gracious! See the bounties of His providence; behold the plenitude of His grace! Will you not love Jehovah because He is Jehovah?

February 28

*O*h! You kind and affectionate hearts who are not rich in wealth but who are rich in love—and that is the world's best wealth—put this golden coin among your silver ones, and it will sanctify them.

The love of Christ does not cast out the love of relatives, but it sanctifies our love and makes them far sweeter. Remember the love of men and women is very sweet. Oh, to have the love of Christ, for His love is as strong as death and mightier than the grave.

The most overpowering thought of all is that He loved us when there was nothing good in us whatever. (See Romans 5:6–8.)

March 1

*H*eaven is a place of complete victory and triumph. This is the battlefield; there is the triumphal procession. This is the land of the sword and the spear; that is the land of the wreath and the crown. Oh, what a thrill of joy will shoot through the hearts of all the blessed when their conquests will be complete in heaven, when death itself—the last of foes—will be slain, when Satan will be dragged captive at the chariot wheels of Christ, when He will have overthrown sin, and when the great shout of universal victory will rise from the hearts of all the redeemed!

March 2

*S*alvation is God's highest glory. He is glorified in every dewdrop that twinkles in the morning sun. He is magnified in every wood flower that blossoms in the copse, although it lives to blush unseen and waste its sweetness in the forest air. But sing, sing, O universe, until you have exhausted yourself; you cannot afford a song so sweet as the song of incarnation. There is more in that than in creation, more melody in Jesus in the manger than there is in worlds on worlds rolling their grandeur round the throne of the Most High.

March 3

*T*he saints in Jesus, when their bodies sleep in peace, have perpetual fellowship with Him— aye, better fellowship than we can enjoy. We have but the transitory glimpse of His face; they gaze upon it every moment. We see Him "through a glass, darkly"; they behold Him "face to face" (1 Cor. 13:12). We sip of the brook by the way; they plunge into the very ocean of unbounded love. We look up sometimes and see our Father smile; look whenever they may, His face is always full of smiles for them. We get some drops of comfort, but they get the honeycomb itself. They are full of peace, full of joy forever. They "sleep in Jesus" (1 Thess. 4:14).

March 4

A city of refuge had round it suburbs of a very great extent. Two thousand cubits were allowed for grazing land for the cattle of the priests, and a thousand cubits within these for fields and vineyards. Now, no sooner did the man reach the outside of the city, the suburbs, than he was safe. It was not necessary for him to get within the walls, but the suburbs themselves were sufficient protection. Learn, hence, that if you do but touch the hem of Christ's garment, you will be made whole. If you do but lay hold of Him with "faith as a grain of mustard seed" (Matt. 17:20), with faith which is scarcely a believing but is truly a believing, you are safe.

March 5

*B*ehold the unpillared arch of heaven. See how it stretches its gigantic span, and yet it falls not though it is unpropped and unbuttressed. "He... hangeth the earth upon nothing" (Job 26:7). What chain is it that binds up the stars and keeps them from falling? A Christian should be a second exhibition of God's universe; his faith should be an unpillared confidence, resting on the past and on the eternity to come as the sure groundwork of its arch. His faith should be like the world; it should hang on nothing but the promise of God, needing nothing to uphold him but the right hand of his Father.

March 6

*O*h, how did heaven wonder! How did the stars stand still with astonishment! And how did the angels stay their songs a moment when for the first time God showed how He might be just and yet be gracious! "Oh, sinner, my heart has devised it. My Son, the pure and perfect, will stand in your stead and be accounted guilty, and you, the guilty, will stand in my Son's stead and be accounted righteous!" It would make us leap upon our feet in astonishment if we did but understand this thoroughly: the wonderful mystery of the transposition of Christ and the sinner.

March 7

*I*f little things have done great things, let us try to do great things also. You know not, you atoms, but that your destiny is sublime. Try and make it so by faith, and the least of you may be mighty through the strength of God. Oh, for grace to trust God! There is no telling what you can do. Spirit of the living God! We want You. You are the life, the soul, and the source of Your people's success. Without You, we can do nothing; with You, we can do everything. (See John 15:5; Philippians 4:13.) "Not by might, nor by power, but by my spirit, saith the LORD" (Zech. 4:6).

March 8

*O*h, who will measure the heights of the Savior's all-sufficiency? First, tell how high is sin, and then, remember that as Noah's flood prevailed over the tops of the earth's mountains, so the flood of Christ's redemption prevails over the tops of the mountains of our sins. In heaven's courts there are today men that once were sinners, but they have been washed—they have been sanctified. Ask them from where the brightness of their robes has come and where their purity has been achieved, and they, with united breath, will tell you that they have washed their robes and made them white in the blood of the Lamb.

March 9

*I*t will not save me to know that Christ is a Savior, but it will save me to trust Him to be my Savior. I will not be delivered from the wrath to come by believing that His atonement is sufficient, but I will be saved by making that atonement my trust, my refuge, and my all. The pith, the essence of faith lies in this: a casting oneself on the promise. It is not the life buoy on board ship that saves the man when he is drowning, nor is it his belief that it is an excellent and successful invention. No, he must have it around his loins, or his hand upon it, or else he will sink.

March 10

*Y*ou see yonder ship. After a long voyage, it has neared the haven but is much injured; the sails are rent to ribbons. That is like the righteous being scarcely saved. But do you see that other ship? It has made a prosperous voyage, and now, laden to the water's edge with the sails all up and with the white canvas filled with the wind, it rides into the harbor joyously and nobly. That is an "abundant entrance." If you and I are helped by God's Spirit to add to our faith virtue and so on (see 2 Peter 1:5–7), we will at the last enter "abundantly into the everlasting kingdom of our Lord and Saviour Jesus Christ" (2 Pet. 1:11).

March 11

*D*ear friends, the last song in this world, the song of triumph, will be full of God and of no one else. Here you praise the instrument. Today you look on this man and on that, and you say, "Thank God for this minister and for this man!" But in that day, forgotten will their names be for a season, even as the stars refuse to shine when the sun himself appears. The song will be to Jehovah, and Jehovah only: "Unto him that loved us, and washed us from our sins in his own blood...to him be glory and dominion for ever and ever. Amen" (Rev. 1:5–6).

March 12

*W*hen no eye sees you except the eye of God, when darkness covers you, when you are shut up from the observation of mortals, even then be like Jesus Christ. Remember His ardent piety, His secret devotion—how, after laboriously preaching the whole day, He stole away in the midnight shades to cry for help from His God. Recollect how His entire life was constantly sustained by fresh inspirations of the Holy Spirit which were derived by prayer. Take care of your secret life; let it be such that you will not be ashamed to have it be read at the last great day.

March 13

*T*he death of the saints is precious in the sight of the Lord. On their account we have cause rather to rejoice than to weep. Yes, we have the fond and firm persuasion that already their redeemed spirits have flown up to the eternal throne. We do believe that they are at this moment joining in the hallelujahs of paradise, feasting on the fruits of the tree of life, and walking by the side of the "river, the streams whereof shall make glad the city of God" (Ps. 46:4). We know they are supremely blessed. We think of them as glorified spirits above who are present with the Lord Jesus.

March 14

*S*ome of you have lost your friends. Come to the grave of your best friend—your brother, yes, one who "sticketh closer than a brother" (Prov. 18:24). Come to the grave of you dearest relative, Christian, for Jesus is your husband: "Thy Maker is thine husband; the LORD of hosts is his name" (Isa. 54:5). Does not affection draw you? Do not the sweet lips of love woo you? Is not the place sanctified where one so well beloved steps, although but for a moment? Surely you need no eloquence. You have the power, in simple but earnest accents, to repeat the words, "Come, see the place where the Lord lay" (Matt. 28:6).

March 15

O h," cries one, "I wish I could escape the wrath of the law! Oh, that I knew that Christ did keep the law for me!" Stop, then, and I will tell you. Do you feel today that you are guilty, lost, and ruined? Do you, with tears in your eyes, confess that none but Jesus can do you good? Are you willing to give up all trusts and cast yourself alone on Him who died upon the cross? Can you look to Calvary and see the bleeding sufferer, all crimson with streams of gore? Then He kept the law for you, and the law cannot condemn those whom Christ has absolved.

March 16

T he Bible is a vein of pure gold, unalloyed by quartz or any earthly substance. This is a star without a speck, a sun without a blot, a light without darkness, a moon without its paleness, and a glory without a dimness. O Bible! It cannot be said of any other book that it is perfect and pure, but of the Bible we can declare that all wisdom is gathered up in it without a particle of folly. This is the judge that ends the strife where wit and reason fail. This is the Book untainted by any error but is pure, unalloyed, perfect truth.

March 17

*P*oor sinner, do take heart, and remember God knows, as we know not, where you are. If you are in the deepest pit in the forest, His almighty eye can see to the bottom. Yes, and in one of the favored moments of the day of salvation—that time accepted—He will send home a promise so sweetly that all your fetters will break off in an instant, your night will be scattered, your dawn begun. And, He will give you "the oil of joy for mourning, the garment of praise for the spirit of heaviness" (Isa. 61:3). Believe now, and you will be comforted now, for the time of faith is the time of comfort.

March 18

*N*o inferior hand has sketched even so much as the most minute parts of providence. It was all marked out, designed, and planned by the mind of the all-wise, all-knowing God. Hence, not even Christ's death was exempt from it. He that wings an angel and guides a sparrow, He that counts the hairs of our heads, was not likely, when He took notice of such little things, to omit the greatest wonder of earth's miracles, the death of Christ. No, the blood-stained page of that Book, the page which makes both past and future glorious with golden words—that blood-stained page, I say—was as much written by Jehovah as any other.

March 19

*M*an cannot please God without bringing himself a great amount of happiness. If any man pleases God, it is because God accepts him as His son, gives him the blessings of adoption, pours upon him the bounties of His grace, makes him a blessed man in this life, and insures him a crown of everlasting life which he will wear and which will shine with unfading luster when the wreaths of earth's glory have all been melted away. While, on the other hand, if a man does not please God, he inevitably brings upon himself sorrow and suffering in this life.

March 20

*C*hrist is always the same. Christ's person never changes. Should He come on earth to visit us again, as surely He will, we should find Him the same Jesus, as loving, as approachable, as generous, and as kind. Though He will be arrayed in nobler garments than He wore when first He visited earth, though He will no more be the Man of Sorrows and grief's acquaintance (see Isaiah 53:3), yet He will be the same person, unchanged by all His glories, His triumphs, and His joys. We bless Christ that, amid His heavenly splendors, His person is just the same and His nature unaffected. "Jesus Christ the same yesterday, and to day, and for ever" (Heb. 13:8).

March 21

Canst thou bind the sweet influences of Pleiades, or loose the bands of Orion?—Job 38:31

*H*e looses the bands of Orion, and none but He. What a blessing it is that He can do it! Oh, that He would perform the wonder tonight!

Lord, end my winter, and let my spring begin. I cannot, with all my longings, raise my soul out of her death and dullness, but all things are possible with You. I need celestial influences, the clear shining of Your love, the beams of Your grace, and the light of Your countenance. These are the Pleiades to me. I suffer much from sin and temptation; these are my wintry signs, my terrible Orion. Lord, work wonders in me and for me. Amen.

March 22

*D*id you ever think of the love which Christ will manifest to you when He will present you without spot or blemish or any such thing before His Father's throne? (See Ephesians 5:27; Jude 1:24.) Well, pause and remember that He loves you at this hour as much as He will love you then, for He will be the same forever as He is today, and He is the same today as He will be forever. (See Hebrews 13:8.) "As the Father hath loved me, so have I loved you" (John 15:9), and a higher degree of love we cannot imagine. The Father loves his Son infinitely, and even so today, believer, does the Son of God love you.

March 23

*C*hildren of God, death has lost its sting. It is sweet to die, to lie upon the breast of Christ and have one's soul kissed out of one's body by the lips of divine affection. And you that have lost friends or that may be bereaved, sorrow not as those who are without hope (1 Thess. 4:13). What a sweet thought the death of Christ brings us concerning those who are departed! They are gone, my brothers, but do you know how far they have gone? The distance between the glorified spirits in heaven and the militant saints on earth seems great, but it is not so. We are not far from home.

March 24

*T*here is one great event which every day attracts more admiration than do the sun and moon and stars. That event is the death of our Lord Jesus Christ. To it the eyes of all the saints who lived before the Christian era were always directed, and backwards, through the thousand years of history, the eyes of all modern saints are looking. Upon Christ the angels in heaven perpetually gaze. "Which things the angels desire to look into" (1 Pet. 1:12), said the apostle. Upon Christ, the eyes of the redeemed are perpetually fixed, and thousands of pilgrims, through this world of tears, have no higher object for their faith.

March 25

*Y*ou have sometimes seen how the ship cuts through the billows, leaving a white furrow behind her and causing the sea to boil around her. Such is life, says Job, "as the swift ships" (Job 9:26). I cannot stop its motion. I may direct it with the rudder of God's Holy Spirit; nevertheless, like a swift ship, my life must speed on its way until it reaches its haven. Where is that haven to be? Will it be found in the land of bitterness and barrenness, that dreary region of the lost? Or will it be that sweet haven of eternal peace?

March 26

*T*he holiest men, the most free from impurity, have always felt it most. He whose garments are the whitest will best perceive the spots upon them. He whose crown shines the brightest will know when he has lost a jewel. He who gives the most light to the world will always be able to discover his own darkness. The angels of heaven veil their faces, and the angels of God on earth, His chosen people, must always veil their faces with humility when they think of what they were.

As you grow downward in humility seek also to grow upward, having nearer approaches to God in prayer and more intimate fellowship with Jesus.

Oh, there is nothing that can so advantage you, nothing that can so prosper you, so assist you, so make you walk towards heaven rapidly, so keep your head upwards towards the sky and your eyes radiant with glory, like the imitation of Jesus Christ. It is when, by the power of the Holy Spirit, you are enabled to walk with Jesus in His very footsteps and tread in His ways that you are most happy and are most known to be the sons of God. For your sake, my brothers, I say, be like Christ.

To draw Him nearer to me, and myself nearer to Him, is the innermost longing of my soul.

March 28

He that loves much must weep much; much love and much sorrow must go together in this vale of tears. Oftentimes, tears are the index of strength. There are periods when they are the noblest thing in the world. The tears of penitents are precious; a cup of them is worth a king's ransom. It is no sign of weakness when a man weeps for sin. It shows that he has strength of mind—no, more—that he has strength imparted by God which enables him to forswear his lusts and overcome his passions and to turn to God with full purpose of heart.

March 29

*O*h, my heart, I bid you now put your treasure where you can never lose it. Put it in Christ; put all your affections in His person, all your hope in His glory, all your trust in His effectual blood, all your joy in His presence, and then you will have put yourself and put your all where you can never lose anything because it is secure. Go, tell your secrets to that "friend that sticketh closer than a brother" (Prov. 18:24). My heart, I charge you, trust all your concerns with Him who can never be taken from you, who will never let you leave Him, even "Jesus Christ the same yesterday, and to day, and for ever" (Heb. 13:8).

March 30

*I*f any of you desire to be saved by works, remember one sin will spoil your righteousness, one dust of this earth's rubbish will spoil the beauty of that perfect righteousness which God requires at your hands. If you would be saved by works, you must be as holy as the angels, you must be as pure and as immaculate as Jesus, for the law requires perfection.

The power to receive is scarcely a power, and yet it is the only power needed for salvation. Come along and take what Christ freely gives you.

Believe in the Lord Jesus Christ, and believe intensely.

*T*hose who do not have to work hard think they will love heaven as a place of service. That is very true. But to the working man, to the man who toils with his brain or with his hands, it must ever be a sweet thought that there is a land where we will rest. Oh, weary sons and daughters of Adam, you will be still, you will be quiet, you will rest yourselves, for all are rich in heaven, all are happy there, all are peaceful. Toil, trouble, travail, and labor are words that cannot be spelled in heaven; they have no such things there, for they always rest.

April 1

*C*ome, see the place where the Lord lay" (Matt. 28:6). Surely you need no argument to move your feet in the direction of the holy sepulcher, but still we will use the utmost power to draw your spirit toward that place. Ask me the greatest man who ever lived—I tell you the Man, Christ Jesus, was "anointed...with the oil of gladness above thy fellows" (Heb. 1:9). If you seek a chamber honored as the resting place of Jesus, turn in at that place; if you would worship at the grave of holiness, come here; if you would see the hallowed spot, come with me, Christian, to that quiet garden, hard by the walls of Jerusalem.

April 2

*C*oming to Christ is just the one essential thing for a sinner's salvation. He that does not come to Christ is yet "in the gall of bitterness, and in the bond of iniquity" (Acts 8:23). Coming to Christ is the very first effect of regeneration. No sooner is the soul quickened than it at once discovers its lost estate, looks out for a refuge, and, believing Christ to be the only one, flies to Him and reposes in Him. Where there is not this coming to Christ, it is certain that there is as yet no quickening. Where there is no quickening, the soul is dead in trespasses and sins; being dead, it cannot enter into the kingdom of heaven.

April 3

*S*inner, unconverted sinner, you have often tried to save yourself, but you have often failed. You have, by your own power and might, sought to curb your evil passions and sins. With you, I lament that all your efforts have been unsuccessful. And I warn you, it will be unsuccessful, for you can never by your own might save yourself. With all the strength you have, you can never regenerate your own soul; you can never cause yourself to be born again. And though the new birth is absolutely necessary, it is absolutely impossible to you unless God the Spirit will do it.

April 4

*P*rayer is the certain forerunner of salvation. Sinner, you cannot pray and perish; prayer and perishing are two things that never go together. I ask you not what your prayer is. It may be a groan, it may be a tear, but if it is a prayer from the inmost heart, you will be saved. Yet, if from your heart you have learned to pray—

> Prayer is the breath of God in man,
> Returning whence it came.

—you cannot perish with God's breath in you. "Whosoever shall call on the name of the Lord shall be saved" (Acts 2:21).

April 5

*L*et not your exertions end in tears, mere weeping will do nothing without action. Get on your feet, you that have voices and might. Go forth and preach the Gospel. Preach it in every street and lane of this huge city. You that have wealth, go forth and spend it for the poor and sick and needy and dying and uneducated and unenlightened. You that have time, go forth and spend it in deeds of goodness. You that have power in prayer, go forth and pray. Everyone to his post, everyone of you to your gun in this day of battle, now for God and for His truth, for God and for the right. Let everyone of us who knows the Lord seek to fight under His banner!

April 6

*B*y the sweet drawing of the Spirit, sinners find "the peace of God, which passeth all understanding, [which keeps their] hearts and minds through Christ Jesus" (Phil. 4:7). Now, you will plainly perceive that all this may be done without any compulsion. Man is as much drawn willingly as if he were not drawn at all, and he comes to Christ with full consent, with as full a consent as if no secret influence had ever been exercised in his heart. But that influence must be exercised, or else there never has been and there never will be any man who either can or will come to the Lord Jesus Christ.

April 7

I will help you. That is very little for Me to do, to help you. Consider what I have done already. What, not help you? Why, I bought you with My blood. What! Not help you? I have died for you, and if I have done the greater, will I not do the less? Help you, My beloved! It is the least thing I will ever do for you. I have done more, and I will do more. Before the day-star first began to shine, I chose you. "I will help thee" (Isa. 41:10, 13, 14). I made the covenant for you and exercised all the wisdom of My eternal mind in the plan of salvation. "I will help thee."

April 8

C hrist longed for the cross because He looked for it as the goal of all His exertions. He could never say, "It is finished" (John 19:30), on His throne, but on His cross He did cry it. He preferred the sufferings of Calvary to the honors of the multitude who crowded round about Him, for bless and heal them as He might, still His work was undone. "I long for My sufferings, because they will be the completion of My great work of grace." It is the end that brings the honor; it is the victory that crowns the warrior rather than the battle. And so Christ longed for this, His death, that He might see the completion of His labor.

April 9

Can you think what must have been the greatness of the atonement which was the substitution for all the agony that God would have cast upon us, if He had not poured it upon Christ?

And can you grasp the thought of the greatness of your Savior's mediation when He paid your debt, and paid it all at once, so that there now remains not one farthing of debt owing from Christ's people to their God, except a debt of love. Christ did pay it all so that man would be set free from all punishment through what Jesus has done. Think, then, how great His atonement is if He has done all this.

April 10

The old saying is, "Go from nature up to nature's God," but it is hard working uphill. The best thing is to go from nature's God down to nature. If you once get to nature's God and believe Him and love Him, it is surprising how easy it is to hear music in the waves and songs in the wild whisperings of the winds, to see God everywhere, in the stones, in the rocks, in the rippling brooks, and to hear Him everywhere, in the lowing of cattle, in the rolling of thunders, and in the fury of tempests. Get Christ first. Put Him in the right place, and you will find Him to be the wisdom of God in your own experience.

April 11

Wherever the church is, there is God. God is pleased, in His mercy and condescension, to stoop from the highest heavens to dwell in this lower heaven, the heaven of His church. It is here, among the household of faith, He deigns—let me say it with sacred reverence—to unbend Himself and hold familiar intercourse with those round about Him whom He has adopted into His family. He may be a consuming fire abroad, but when He comes into His own house He is all mercy, mildness, and love. Abroad He does great works of power, but at home in His own house He does great works of grace.

April 12

Many men believe in the existence of a God, but they do not love that belief. But to the Christian, the thought that there is a God is the sunshine of his existence. His intellect bows before the Most High like the angel who prostrates himself because he loves to adore his Maker. His intellect is as fond of God as his imagination. "Oh!" he says, "My God, I bless You that You are, for You are my highest treasure, my richest and my rarest delight. I love You with all my intellect. I have neither thought nor judgment nor conviction nor reason which I do not lay at Your feet and consecrate to Your honor."

April 13

*E*ach of God's saints is sent into the world to prove some part of the divine character. In heaven we will read the great book of the experience of all the saints and gather from that book the whole of the divine character as having been proved and illustrated. Each Christian man is a manifestation and a display of some position or other of God. A different part may belong to each of us, but when the whole will be combined, when all the rays of evidence will be brought, as it were, into one great sun and shine forth with meridian splendor, we will see in Christian experience a beautiful revelation of our God.

April 14

*I*f I once wandered on yonder mountaintop, and Jesus climbed up and caught me and put me on his shoulders and carried me home, I cannot and dare not doubt that He is my Shepherd. If I had belonged to some other sheep owner, He would not have sought me. And from the fact that He did seek, I learn that He must be my Shepherd. Could I trace my deliverance to the hand of a creature, I should think that some creature might be my shepherd; but since he who has been reclaimed of God must confess that God alone has done it, such a one will feel persuaded that the Lord must be his Shepherd because He brought him and delivered him.

April 15

*A*h, if we did but love Christ better, my brothers and sisters, if we lived nearer to the Cross, if we knew more of the value of His blood, if we wept like Him over Jerusalem, if we felt more what it was for souls to perish and what it was for men to be saved—if we did but rejoice with Christ in the prospect of His seeing the travail of His soul and being abundantly satisfied (see Isaiah 53:11)—if we did but delight more in the divine decree that the kingdoms of this world will be given to Christ, I am sure we should all of us find more ways and more means for the sending forth of the Gospel of Christ.

April 16

*H*eaven sings evermore. Before the throne of God, angels and redeemed saints extol His name. And this world is singing too, sometimes with the loud noise of the rolling thunder, of the boiling sea, of the dashing waterfall, and of the lowing cattle, and often with that still, solemn harmony which flows from the vast creation when in its silence it praises God.

In heaven they sing, "The Lord be exalted; let His name be magnified forever." And the earth sings the same: "Great are You in Your works, Lord! And unto You be glory."

April 17

*L*ove for Christ smoothes the path of duty and wings the feet to travel it; it makes the life of sincere devotion.

Love has a clear eye, but it can only see one thing. It is blind to every interest but that of its Lord. It sees things in the light of His glory and weighs actions in the scales of His honor. It counts royalty as drudgery if it cannot reign for Christ, but it delights in servitude as much as in honor if it can thereby advance the Master's kingdom. Its end sweetens all its means; its object lightens its toil and removes its weariness.

April 18

*I*n nature, after evening time there comes night. The sun has had its hour of journeying; the fiery steeds are weary; they must rest. Lo, they descend the azure steeps and plunge their burning hooves in the western sea while night in her ebony chariot follows at their heels. God, however, oversteps the rule of nature. He is pleased to send to His people times when the eye of reason expects to see no more day but fears that the glorious landscape of God's mercies will be shrouded in the darkness of His forgetfulness. But instead, God overleaps nature and declares that "at evening time," instead of darkness, "it shall be light" (Zech. 14:7).

April 19

When Jesus Christ came to build His temple, He found no mountain on which to build it. He had no mountain in our nature. He had to find a mountain in His own, and the mountain upon which He has built His church is the mountain of His own unchangeable affection, His own strong love, and His own omnipotent grace and infallible truthfulness. It is this that constitutes the mountain upon which the church is built, and on this the foundation has been dug and the great stones laid in the trenches with oaths and promises and blood to make them stand secure, even though earth should rock and all creation suffer decay.

April 20

There is none other name under heaven given among men, whereby we must be saved" (Acts 4:12), but "Jesus Christ, and him crucified" (1 Cor. 2:2). There were not two arks but one ark, so there are not two Saviors but one Savior. There was no other means of salvation except the ark, so there is no plan of deliverance except by Jesus Christ, the Savior of sinners. In vain you climb the lofty top of Sinai. In vain you climb to the highest pinnacles of your self-conceit and your worldly merit. You will be drowned, "For other foundation can no man lay than that is laid, which is Jesus Christ" (1 Cor. 3:11).

April 21

O h, newborn soul, trembling with anxiety, if you have not yet beheld the fair face of your Beloved, if you cannot as yet delight in the majesty of His offices and the wonders of His person, let your soul be fully alive to the richness of His grace and the preciousness of His blood. These you have in your possession, the pledges of your interest in Him. Love Him then for these, and in due time He will reveal unto you fresh wonders and glories, so that you will be able to exclaim, "Oh, staff of my life and strength of my heart, I will sit and sing under Your shadow. Yes, I will sing a song of love touching my Well Beloved."

April 22

I t is the highest stage of manhood to have no wish, no thought, no desire, but Christ. It is to feel that to die were bliss if it were for Christ; to feel that to live in penury and woe and scorn and contempt and misery were sweet for Christ; to feel that it matters nothing what becomes of one's self so that our Master is but exalted; to feel that though, like a dried leaf, we are blown in the blast, we are quite without care as to where we are going so long as we feel that the Master's hand is guiding us according to His will.

April 23

*A*ged and mellow saints have so sweet a savor of Christ in them that their conversation is sweetly refreshing to him who delights to hear of the glories of redeeming love. They have tried the anchor in the hour of storm; they have tested the armor in the day of battle; they have proved the shadow of the great rock in the burning noontide in the weary land; therefore, they talk of those things and of Him who is all these to them. We must dive into the same waters if we would bring up the same pearls.

April 24

*A*n honored saint was once so ravished with a revelation of his Lord's love that, feeling his mortal frame to be unable to sustain more of such bliss, he cried, "Hold, Lord, it is enough, it is enough!" In heaven we will be able to put the bottomless well of love to our lips and drink on forever. Ah, that will be love indeed which will overflow our souls forever in our Father's house above! Who can tell the transports, the raptures, the amazements of delight which that love will beget in us? And who can guess the sweetness of the song or the swiftness of the obedience which will be the heavenly expressions of love made perfect?

April 25

*T*he best enjoyments of Christ on earth are but as the dipping of our finger in water for the cooling of our thirst, but heaven is bathing in seas of bliss. Even so, our love here is but one drop of the same substance as the waters of the ocean but not comparable for magnitude or depth. Oh, how sweet it will be to be married to the Lord Jesus and to enjoy forever, and without any interruption, the heavenly delights of His society! Surely, if a glimpse of Him melts our soul, the full fruition of Him will be enough to burn up our hearts with affection.

April 26

*W*hen the soul is led by the Holy Spirit to take a clear view of Jesus in His various offices, how speedily the heart is on fire with love! To see Him stooping from His throne to become man, next yielding to suffering to become man's sympathizing friend, and then bowing to death itself to become his ransom is enough to stir every passion of the soul. To discern Him by faith as the propitiation for sin, sprinkling His own blood within the veil and nailing our sins to His cross, is a sight which never fails to excite the reverent yet rapturous admiration of the beholder.

*C*hrist never lingers long with dumb souls; if there is no crying out to Him, He departs. What a marvelous influence prayer has upon our fellowship with Jesus! We may always measure one by the other. Those who have been constant attendants on the kind Intercessor pray most fervently and frequently, while, on the other hand, those who wrestle the hardest in supplication will hold the angel the longest. Joshua's voice stayed the sun in the heavens for a few hours, but the voice of prayer can detain the Sun of Righteousness for months and even years.

*R*emember that in proportion to the fullness of your heart will be the fullness of your life. Be empty hearted and your life will be a meager skeleton existence. Be full hearted and your life will be full and strong, a thing that will tell upon the world. Keep, then, your peace with God firm within you. Keep yourself close to this, that Jesus Christ has made peace between you and God. And keep your conscience still; then will your heart be full and your soul strong to do your Master's work. Keep your peace with God. This will keep your heart pure.

April 29

*D*o not be afraid. Christ is your strength and righteousness. A wave comes against the side of the ship, but it does not hurt the ship. It only drives the wedges in tighter. The Master is at the helm—will that not assure your heart? It has floated over so many billows—will that not increase your confidence? It must, indeed, be a strong billow that will sink it now; there will never be such a one.

Christ presents the perfect number of all His people to the Father in the last day; not one will perish. The ark of our salvation will bring all its living freight into the haven of everlasting rest.

April 30

*T*his morning our desires go forth for growth in our acquaintance with the Lord Jesus. This was most blessedly perfect long before we had the slightest knowledge of Him. Before we had a being in the world, we had a being in His heart. When we were enemies to Him, He knew us, our misery and our wickedness. When we wept bitterly in despairing repentance and viewed Him only as a judge and a ruler, He viewed us as His well-beloved brothers. He never mistook His chosen but always beheld them as objects of His infinite affection. "The Lord knoweth them that are his" (2 Tim. 2:19).

May 1

*Y*ou have no place in which to pour your troubles except the ear of God. If you tell them to your friends, you only put your troubles out a moment, and they will return again. Roll your burden to God, and you have rolled it into a great deep, out of which it will never by any possibility rise. Cast your troubles where you cast your sins. You have cast your sins into the depths of the sea; there cast your troubles also. Never keep a trouble half an hour on your own mind before you tell it to God. As soon as the trouble comes, quick, the first thing, tell it to your Father.

May 2

*I*s my conscience at peace? For, if my heart condemns me, God is greater than my heart and does know all things (1 John 3:20). If my conscience bears witness with me that I am a partaker of the precious grace of salvation, then happy am I! I am one of those to whom God has given the "peace of God, which passeth all understanding" (Phil. 4:7). Now, why is this called "the peace of God"? Because it comes from God, because it was planned by God, because God gave His Son to make the peace, because God gives His Spirit to give the peace in the conscience, and because, indeed, it is God Himself in the soul.

May 3

Soldier of the Cross, the hour is coming when the note of victory will be proclaimed throughout the world. The battlements of the enemy must soon succumb; the swords of the mighty must soon be given up to the Lord of Lords. What! Soldier of the Cross, in the day of victory would you have it said that you did turn your back in the day of battle? Do you not wish to have a share in the conflict, that you may have a share in the victory? If you have even the hottest part of the battle, will you falter? You will have the brightest part of the victory if you are in the fiercest of the conflict.

May 4

It is often remarked that after soul-sorrow our pastors are more gifted with words in season and their speech is more full of savor. This is to be accounted for by the sweet influence of grief when sanctified by the Holy Spirit. Blessed Redeemer, we delight in Your love, and Your presence is the light of our joys. But if Your brief withdrawals qualify us for glorifying You in cheering Your saints, we thank You for leaving us as we seek You by night. It will somewhat cheer us that You are blessing us when You take away Your richest blessing.

May 5

*I*t certainly is not possible for us to be in a position where Omnipotence cannot assist us. God has servants everywhere. There are "treasures hid in the sand" (Deut. 33:19), and the Lord's chosen shall eat thereof. When the clouds hide the mountains, they are as real as in the sunshine, so the promise and the providence of God are unchanged by the obscurity of our faith or the difficulties of our position. There is hope, and hope at hand; therefore, let us be of good cheer.

When we are at our worst, let us trust with unshaking faith. Recollect that then is the time when we can most glorify God by faith.

May 6

*T*he cross of Christ is Christ's glory. Man seeks to win glory by the sacrifice of others, Christ by the sacrifice of Himself. Men seek to get crowns of gold; He sought a crown of thorns. Men think that glory lies in being exalted over others; Christ thought that His glory did lie in becoming "a worm, and no man" (Ps. 22:6), a scoff and reproach among all that beheld Him. He stooped when He conquered, and He counted that the glory lay as much in the stooping as in the conquest.

Our God has made the "dayspring from on high" (Luke 1:78) to visit us. Our life is bright with these visits as the sky with stars.

May 7

*S*tars may be seen from the bottom of a deep well when they cannot be discerned from the top of a mountain. So are many things learned in adversity which the prosperous man dreams not of. We need affliction as the trees need winter so that we may collect sap and nourishment for future blossoms and fruit. Sorrow is as necessary for the soul as medicine is to the body:

> The path of sorrow, and that path alone,
> Leads to the land where sorrow is unknown.

The adversities of today are a preparatory school for higher learning.

May 8

*W*hen heaven smiles and pours down its showers of grace, then they are precious things, but without the celestial rain we might as much expect water from the arid waste as a real blessing in the use of them. "All my springs are in thee" (Ps. 87:7) is the believer's daily confession to his Lord—a confession which until death must ever be upon his lips. As love comes from heaven, so it must feed on heavenly bread. It cannot exist in the wilderness unless it is fed by manna from on high. Love must feed on love. The very soul and life of our love to God is His love to us.

May 9

*T*he choicest communications ever made of human minds are those which have come from the Great Father. Say, poor soul, what do you get in Christ whenever you go to Him? Can you not say, "Oh! I get more love from Him than I had before. I never approached near to Him without gaining a large draught and ample fill of the love of God." Out of His fullness, we receive grace for grace and love for love. In a word, by faith we, "beholding as in a glass the glory of the Lord, are changed into the same image" (2 Cor. 3:18), and the image of God is love. Live upon Christ, who is the daily manna, and you will live well.

May 10

*O*nly love seeks after love. If I desire the love of another, it can surely only be because I myself have love toward him. We care not to be loved by those whom we do not love. It is an embarrassment rather than an advantage to receive love from those to whom we would not return it. When God asks for human love, it is because God is love. Whatever our mood or feeling, the heart of Jesus is full of love, love which was not caused by our good behavior and is not diminished by our follies, love which is as sure in the night of darkness as in the brightness of the day of joy.

May 11

*I*f you would find God, He dwells on every hilltop and in every valley; God is everywhere in creation. But, if you want a special display of Him, if you would know what the secret place of the tabernacle of the Most High is—the inner chamber of divinity—you must go where you find the church of true believers, for it is here He makes His continual residence known in the hearts of the humble and contrite who tremble at His Word. Every church is to our Lord a more sublime thing than a constellation in the heavens. As He is precious to His saints, so they are precious to Him.

May 12

*W*e love Jesus when we are advanced in the divine life from a participation with Him in the great work of His incarnation. We long to see our fellowmen turned from darkness to light, and we love Him as the Sun of Righteousness who alone can illuminate them. We hate sin, and therefore we rejoice in Him as manifested to take away sin. We yearn for holier and happier times, and therefore we adore Him as the coming Ruler of all lands who will bring a millennium with Him in the day of His appearing. Love the soul of every man with all the intensity of your being.

May 13

*T*here was never a soul yet that sincerely sought the Savior who perished before he found Him. No, the gates of death will never shut on you until the gates of grace have opened for you. Until Christ has washed your sins away, you will never be baptized in Jordan's flood. Your life is secure, for this is God's constant plan: He keeps His own elect alive until the day of His grace, and then He takes them to Himself. And inasmuch as you know your need of a Savior, you are one of His, and you will never die until you have found Him. God sends the right messenger to the right man.

May 14

*W*e love him, because he first loved us" (1 John 4:19). Here is the starting point of love's race. This is the rippling rill which afterwards swells into a river, the torch with which the pile of piety is kindled. The emancipated spirit loves the Savior for the freedom which He has conferred upon it. It beholds the agony with which the priceless gift was purchased, and it adores the bleeding Sufferer for the pains which He so generously endured.

On taking a survey of our whole lives, we see that the kindness of God has run all through it like a silver thread.

May 15

*I*f Christ is more excellent at one time than another it certainly is in "the cloudy and dark day" (Ezek. 34:12). We can never so well see the true color of Christ's love as in the night of weeping. Christ in the dungeon, Christ on the bed of sickness, Christ in poverty is Christ indeed to a sanctified man. No vision of Christ Jesus is so truly a revelation as that which is seen in the Patmos of suffering. This He proves to His beloved, not by mere words of promise but by actual deeds of affection. As our sufferings abound, so He makes our consolations to abound.

May 16

*S*unlight is never more grateful than after a long watch in the midnight blackness. Christ's presence is never more acceptable than after a time of weeping on account of His departure. It is a sad thing that we should need to lose our mercies to teach us to be grateful for them. Let us mourn over this crookedness of our nature, and let us strive to express our thankfulness for mercies so that we may not have to lament their removal. If you desire Christ for a perpetual guest, give Him all the keys of your heart. Let not one cabinet be locked up from Him. Give Him the range of every room and the key to every chamber; thus, you will constrain Him to remain.

May 17

We never live so well as when we live on the Lord Jesus simply as He is and not upon our enjoyments and raptures. Faith is never more likely to increase in strength than in times which seem adverse to her. When she is lightened of trust in joys, experiences, moods, feelings, and the like, she rises nearer to heaven. Trust in your Redeemer's strength, you benighted soul. Exercise what faith you have, and by and by He will rise upon you with healings beneath His wings. Go from faith to faith, and you will receive blessing upon blessing.

May 18

Just so far as the Lord will give us grace to suffer for Christ and to suffer with Christ, just so far does He honor us. Afflictions cannot sanctify us except as they are used by Christ as His mallet and His chisel. Our joys and our efforts cannot make us ready for heaven apart from the hand of Jesus who fashions our hearts aright and prepares us to be partakers of the inheritance of the saints in light. Our griefs cannot mar the melody of our praise; we reckon them to be the bass part of our life's song. This vale of tears is but the pathway to the better country; this world of woe is but the stepping-stone to a world of bliss.

May 19

*C*onsider the history of the Redeemer's love, and a thousand enchanting acts of affection will suggest themselves, all of which have had for their design the weaving of the heart into Christ and the intertwining of the thoughts and emotions of the renewed soul with the mind of Jesus. Nearness of life towards the Lamb will necessarily involve greatness of love for Him. As nearness to the sun increases the temperature of the various planets, so close communion with Jesus raises the heat of affections towards Him. This alone is the true life of a Christian—its source, its sustenance, its fashion, its end—all gathered up in one name, Christ Jesus.

May 20

*C*hoice discoveries of the wondrous love and grace of Jesus are most tenderly granted to believers in the times of grief. Then it is that He lifts them up from His feet, where, like Mary, it is their delight to sit, and exalts them to the position of the favored John, pressing them to His breast and bidding them lean on His bosom.

The love of Christ in its sweetness, its fullness, its greatness, and its faithfulness passes all human comprehension.

Heaven on earth is abounding love to Jesus. This is the first and last of true delight—to love Him who is "the first and the last" (Rev. 22:13). To love Jesus is another name for paradise.

*P*rayer is the lisping of the believing infant, the shout of the fighting believer, the requiem of the dying saint falling asleep in Jesus. It is the breath, the watchword, the comfort, the strength, and the honor of a Christian.

Spiritual mercies are good things, and not only good things but the best things, so that you may well ask for them. For if "no good thing will be withheld" (Ps. 84:11), more importantly, none of the best things will be withheld.

If you want power in prayer, you must have purity in life.

If our faith is to grow exceedingly, we must maintain constant intercourse with God.

May 22

A Christian ought to be a comforter with kind words on his lips and sympathy in his heart. He should carry sunshine wherever he goes and diffuse happiness around him. If you see Jesus and abide in the light of His countenance habitually, your faces, your characters, and your lives will grow resplendent even without your knowing it. If the tender mercy of God has visited us and done so much more for us than I can tell or than you can hear, let us ourselves exhibit tender mercy in our dealings with our fellowmen. He who is the means of imparting spiritual life to others lives most and lives best.

May 23

A clear proof of the divine origin of Scripture is afforded by its portrait of the perfect man. Jesus is sinless in thought, word, and deed. His enemies are unable to find a fault in Him either of excess or defect. Nowhere else in the world have we such another portrait of man. It would be superfluous to say that nowhere have we such another man. Jesus is unique; He is original, with peculiarities all His own but without any divergence from the straight line of moral virtue. He is not a recluse, whose character would have few relationships and therefore few tests, but one living in the fierce light of a king among men, coming into relation with the world in a thousand ways.

May 24

C oncerning the consciousness of evil in the past of our lives and the tendency to wrongdoing in our nature, the Bible is very clear. It is most admirably explicit as to God's way of removing this barrier to our future progress. In Holy Scripture, we see a most wise and gracious method for the putting away of guilt without injury to the divine justice. The atonement offered by the Lord Jesus, who is the essence of the revelation of God, is an eminently satisfactory solution of the soul's sternest problem. Our feeling is that God, the universal Ruler, must do right and must not, even for mercy's sake, relax the rule that evil done must bring evil as its consequence.

*I*t has been well said, "meadows may be occasionally flooded, but the marshes are drowned by the tide at every return thereof."

There is all this difference between the sins of the righteous and those of the ungodly. Surprised by temptation, true saints are flooded with a passing outburst of sin, but the wicked delight in transgression and live in it as in their element. The saint in his errors is a star under a cloud, but the sinner is darkness itself. The gracious may fall into iniquity, but the graceless run into it, wallow in it, and again and again return to it.

May 26

*B*etween the revelation of God in His Word and that in His works, there can be no actual discrepancy. The one may go farther than the other, but the revelation must be harmonious. Between the interpretation of the works and the interpretation of the Word, there may be very great differences. It must be admitted that scholars of the Book have sometimes missed its meaning. No, more—it is certain that, in their desire to defend their Bible, devout persons have been unwise enough to twist its words. If they had always labored to understand what God said in His Book and had steadfastly adhered to its meaning, they would have been wise.

May 27

*W*e may not refuse reliance upon God on the ground of our insignificance, for it is not conceivable that anything can be too little for God. The wonders of the microscope are quite as remarkable as those of the telescope; we may not set a boundary to the Lord in one direction any more than in the other. He can and will show His divine skill in a man's life as well as in a planet's circuit.

Witnesses are alive to testify of the Lord's making bare His arm on the behalf of them that trust Him. (See Isaiah 52:10; 2 Chronicles 16:9.) Any man may also put the principle to the test in his own instance, and it is memorable that none have done so in vain.

May 28

*I*t has been asserted that God cannot be known. Those who say this declare that they themselves know nothing but phenomena.

He who made the world was certainly an intelligent being, in fact the highest intelligence, for in a myriad of ways His works display the presence of profound thought and knowledge. Lord Bacon said, "I had rather believe all the fables of the Talmud and the Koran than that this universal frame is without a mind." This being so, we do in that very fact know God in a measure and in such a measure that we are prepared to trust Him. He that made all things is more truly an object of confidence than all things that He has made.

*S*elf-reliance is instilled as a moral virtue, and in a certain sense, with due surroundings, it is so. Observation and experience show that it is a considerable force in the world. He who questions his own powers and does not know his own mind hesitates, trembles, falters, and fails. His diffidence is the author of his disappointment The self-reliant individual hopes, considers, plans, resolves, endeavors, perseveres, and succeeds. His assurance of victory is one leading cause of his triumph. A man believes in his own capacity, and unless he is altogether a piece of emptiness, he gradually convinces others that his estimate is correct.

May 30

*B*eloved reader, what is your desperate case? What heavy matter have you in hand this evening? Bring it here. The God of the prophets lives, and lives to help His saints. He will not suffer you to lack any good thing. Believe in the Lord of Hosts! Approach Him pleading the name of Jesus. You too will see the finger of God working marvels for His people. "According to your faith be it unto you" (Matt. 9:29). In our hours of bodily pain and mental anguish, we find ourselves as naturally driven to prayer as the wreck is driven upon the shore by the waves.

We then choose faith rather than doubt as the mainspring of our lives.

*P*rayer must not be our random work but our daily business, our habit, and our vocation. As artists give themselves to their models, and poets to their classical pursuits, so must we surrender ourselves to prayer. We must be immersed in prayer as in our element and so "pray without ceasing" (1 Thess. 5:17). Lord, teach us to pray that we may be more prevalent in supplication.

The common fault with the most of us is our readiness to yield to distractions. Our thoughts go roving hither and thither, and we make little progress towards our desired end. Like quicksilver, our minds will not hold together but roll off this way and that. How great an evil this is! It injures us, and, what is worse, it insults our God.

June 1

One of the marvels of the Bible is its singular fullness. It is not a book of gold leaf beaten thin, as most books pertaining to thought are, but its sentences are nuggets of unalloyed truth. The Book of God is clearly the god of books, for it is infinite. A German author well said, "In this little Book is contained all the wisdom of the world."

> We search the world for truth; we cull
>   The good, the pure, the beautiful
> From graven stone and written scroll
>   From all old flower fields of the soul;
> And, weary seekers of the best
>   We come back laden from the quest,
> To find that all the sages said
>   Is in the Book our mothers read.

June 2

It has been well said, "Nothing is easier than to doubt. A man of moderate ability or learning can doubt more than the wisest men believe." Faith demands knowledge, for it is an intelligent grace, able and anxious to justify itself. But, infidelity is not required to give a reason for the doubt that is in it; a defiant demeanor and a blustering tone answer its purpose. The zenith of unbelief is to know nothing. What is this but the glorification of ignorance?

A man may glide into agnosticism insensibly, and remain in it languidly, but to believe is to be alive. Those who think faith is a childish business will have to make considerable advances toward manliness before they are able to test their own theories.

June 3

*T*he most important part of human life is not its
end but its beginning. Our death day is the
child of the past, but our opening years are the sires
of the future. At the last hour men summon to their
bedside a solemnity of thought which arrives too
late for any practical result. The hush and awe and
faraway look, so frequent in departing moments,
should have come much sooner. Commend us to the
example of the Hebrew king who fasted and wore
sackcloth while the child was yet alive. Wisely did he
foresee the uselessness of lamenting when the scene
should close. "Can I bring him back again?" (2 Sam.
12:23) is one of the most serious of questions.

June 4

*L*aden boughs hang low. The nettle mounts
above its fellow weeds, but the violet lies
shrouded under its leaves and is only found out by
its own scent.

Walking one day by a stream, we were conscious of a delicious perfume, and only then did we
perceive the little blue eyes which were looking up
to us so meekly from the ground on which we stood.
Virtue is always modest, and modesty is itself a virtue. He who is discovered by his real excellence, and
not by his egotistical advertisements of his own per-
fections, is a man worth knowing.

June 5

*Y*ou may have sunk low in despondency, and even despair, but if your soul has any longing towards Christ, and if you are seeking to rest in His finished work, God sees the light. He not only sees it, but He also preserves it in you. "I the LORD do keep it" (Isa. 27:3). Sometimes we cannot see the light, but God always sees the light; that is much better than our seeing it. If the Lord has given you light, dear reader, He looks on that light with peculiar interest. Not only is it dear to Him as His own handiwork, but it is like Himself, for "God is light" (1 John 1:5).

June 6

*M*any can bring the Scriptures to the mind, but the Lord alone can prepare the mind to receive the Scriptures. Our Lord Jesus differs from all other teachers. They reach the ear, but He instructs the heart. They deal with the outward letter, but He imparts an inward taste for the truth by which we perceive its savor and spirit. The most unlearned of men become ripe scholars in the school of grace when the Lord Jesus by His Holy Spirit unfolds the mysteries of the kingdom to them and grants the divine anointing by which they are enabled to behold the invisible. Happy are we if we have had our understandings cleared and strengthened by the Master!

June 7

*W*e are never out of the reach of temptation. Both at home and abroad we are liable to meet with allurements to evil. The morning opens with peril, and the shades of evening find us still in jeopardy. They whom God keeps are well-kept, but woe unto those who go forth into the world or even dare to walk around their own houses unarmed. Those who think themselves secure are more exposed to danger than any others. The armor bearer of sin is self-confidence. Be not secure. We need a watchman for the night as well as a guardian for the day. Oh, for the constraining love of Jesus to keep us active and useful!

June 8

*W*hen the beams of the sun are focused upon one spot by a magnifying glass, then they cause fire. Likewise, when our thoughts are concentrated on one object, they warm the heart and at last burn the truth into it.

There are many rays of light, but they are scattered. We look a little upon many things while what is wanted is one great truth and so much attention upon it as will fix it on the heart and set the soul blazing with it. This is the fault of many lives; they are squandered upon a dozen objects, whereas if they were economized for one, they would be mighty lives known in the present and honored in the future.

June 9

*T*he unsoundness of a vessel is not seen when it is empty but when it is filled with water; then we will see whether it will leak or not.

It is in our prosperity that we are tested. Men are not fully discovered to themselves until they are tried by the fullness of success. Praise finds pride, wealth reveals selfishness, and learning discovers the leak of unbelief. Success is the crucible of character. Hence, the prosperity which some welcome as an unmixed favor may far more rightly be regarded as an intense form of testing. Oh, Lord, preserve us when we are full as much as when we are empty.

June 10

A garrison is not free from danger while it has an enemy lodged within. You may bolt all your doors and fasten all your windows, but if the thieves have placed even a little child within doors who can draw the bolts for them, the house is still unprotected. All the sea outside a ship cannot do it damage until the water enters within and fills the hold. Hence, it is clear our greatest danger is from within. All the devils in hell and tempters on earth could do us no injury if there were no corruption in our nature. Alas, our hearts are our greatest enemies; these are the little home-born thieves.

*W*e are not exacting when we demand that each sincere man should read the Bible for himself. In testing a book which professes to be the revelation of God's mind, we will act unworthily if we trust to others, be they who they may. Secondhand information lacks assurance and vividness; a personal investigation is far more satisfactory and beneficial. Many other books have been warmly praised by their readers, but we have never yet met with any other volume which has commanded such frequent enthusiasm and such devoted affection as the Bible. Neither have we heard of one which answers so many and such diverse purposes in connection with the lives of men.

June 12

*C*hrist had no transgressions of His own. He took ours upon His head. He never committed a wrong, but He took all my sin, and all yours, if you are a believer. Concerning all His people, it is true, He bore their griefs and carried their sorrows in His own body on the tree. (See Isaiah 53:4; 1 Peter 2:24.) Sin may drag you ever so low, but Christ's great atonement is still under all. You may have descended into the deeps, but you cannot have fallen so low as the uttermost, and "to the uttermost" (Heb. 7:25) He saves.

Today the world's one and only remedy is the Cross.

June 13

We do not observe God's hand as much as we should. Our good puritan forefathers, when it rained, used to say that God had unstopped the bottles of heaven. When it rains nowadays, we think the clouds have become condensed. If they had a field of hay cut, they used to plead to the Lord that He would bid the sun to shine. We, perhaps, are wiser as we think, and we consider it hardly worthwhile to pray about such things, thinking they will come in the course of nature. They believed that God was in every storm, in every cloud of dust. They used to speak of a present God in everything.

June 14

How is the world to be brought back? How is it to be restored? How is this to be? We answer: the reason why there was an original harmony between earth and heaven was because there was love between them both. Our great reason for hoping that there will be at last an undiscordant harmony between heaven and earth reestablished is simply this, that God has already manifested His love toward us (see Romans 5:8), and that in return, hearts touched by His grace do even now love Him. When they will be multiplied and love reestablished, then will harmony be complete.

June 15

*L*osses are frequently the means God uses to fetch home His wandering sheep. Like fierce dogs, they bring wanderers back to the Shepherd How often have we seen the Christian rendered obedient to his Lord's will by the honest goodness of bread and hard labor. When rich and increased with goods, many professors carry their heads much too loftily and speak much too boastfully. Like David, they boast: "My mountain stands fast; it will never be moved." (See Psalm 30:6–7.) When the Christian grows wealthy, is in good repute, and has good health and a happy family, he too often wanders away. If he is a true child of God, there is a rod prepared for him.

June 16

*F*riendship is the only thing in the world concerning the usefulness of which all mankind is agreed. Friendship seems as necessary an element of a comfortable existence in this world as fire and water, or even air itself. A man may drag along a miserable existence in proud solitary dignity, but his life is scarcely life. It is nothing but an existence, the tree of life being stripped of the leaves of hope and the fruits of joy. He who would be happy here must have friends, and he who would be happy hereafter, must, above all things, find a friend in the world to come in the person of God, the Father of His people.

June 17

Sometimes Saul was among the prophets, easily turning into a prophet, and then afterwards among the witches. Sometimes he was in one place and then another and insincere in everything. How many such we have in every Christian assembly, men who are very easily molded. They have affectionate dispositions, very likely a tender conscience, but then the conscience is so remarkably tender that when touched it seems to give, and you are afraid to probe deeper. It heals as soon as it is wounded. You may press them whichever way you wish; they are so elastic you can always effect your purpose. But then, they are not fixed in character and soon return to be what they were before.

June 18

Abide with us: for...the day is far spent" (Luke 24:29). Beloved, remember what you have heard of your Lord Jesus and what He has done for you; make your heart the golden pot of manna to preserve the memorial of the heavenly bread whereon you have fed in days gone by. Let your memory treasure up everything about Christ which you have either felt or known or believed, and then let your fond affections hold Him fast forevermore. Love the person of your Lord! Bring forth the alabaster box of your heart, even though it is broken, and let all the precious ointment of your affection come streaming on His pierced feet.

June 19

*P*ray for God to send a few men with what the Americans call "grit" in them; men who, when they know a thing to be right, will not turn away or turn aside or stop; men who will persevere all the more because there are difficulties to meet or foes to encounter; men who stand all the more true to their Master because they are opposed; men who, the more they are thrust into the fire, the hotter they become; men who, just like the bow, the further the string is drawn, the more powerfully it sends forth its arrows. The more such men are trodden upon, the mightier they will become in the cause of truth against error.

June 20

*R*eturn unto thy rest, O my soul; for the LORD hath dealt bountifully with thee" (Ps. 116:7). It was at the still hour, when the gates of the day were closing, that with weary wing the dove came back to her master. O Lord, enable me this evening thus to return to Jesus. The dove could not endure to spend a night hovering over the restless waste, nor can I bear to be even for another hour away from Jesus, the rest of my heart, the home of my spirit. She did not merely alight upon the roof of the ark, she "came in to him" (Gen. 8:11). Even so would my longing spirit look into the secret of the Lord, pierce to the interior of truth, enter into that which is within the veil, and reach to my Beloved in very deed.

*F*aithfulness to us in our faults is a certain sign of fidelity in a friend. (See Proverbs 27:6.) You may depend upon that man who will tell you of your faults in a kind and considerate manner. Give me for a friend a man who will speak honestly of me before my face, who will not tell first one neighbor and then another but who will come straight to my house and say, "I feel there is a wrong in you, my brother, I must tell you of." That man is a true friend; he has proved himself to be so, for we never get any praise for telling people of their faults. We rather hazard their dislike. A man will sometimes thank you for it, but he does not often like you any the better.

June 22

*W*hat we are taught to seek or shun in prayer, we should equally pursue or avoid in action. Very earnestly, therefore, should we avoid temptation, seeking to walk guardedly in the path of obedience. We are not to enter the thicket in search of the lion. This lion may cross our path or leap upon us from the thicket, but we have nothing to do with hunting him. He that meets with him, even though he wins the day, will find it a stern struggle. Let the Christian pray that he may be spared the encounter. Our Savior, who had experience of what temptation meant, thus earnestly admonished his disciples: "Pray that ye enter not into temptation" (Luke 22:40).

June 23

You know in a wheel there is one portion that never turns round, that stands steadfast, and that is the axle. So, in God's providence there is an axle which never moves. Christian, here is a sweet thought for you. Your state is ever changing. Sometimes you are exalted and sometimes depressed, yet there is an unmoving point in your state. What is that axle? What is the pivot upon which all the machinery revolves? It is the axle of God's everlasting love towards His covenant people. The exterior of the wheel is changing, but the center stands forever fixed. Other things may move, but God's love never moves. It is the axle of the wheel and will endure.

June 24

First, then, here is what they are to tell. It is to be a story of personal experience. "Go home to thy friends, and tell them how great things the Lord hath done for thee, and hath had compassion on thee" (Mark 5:19). Do not tell what you have believed but what you have felt, what you really know to be your own. Do not tell what great things you have read but what great things the Lord has done for you. Tell not only what you have seen done in the great congregation and how great sinners have turned to God, but tell what the Lord has do⁻ for you. And mark this: there is never a more interesting story than that which a man tells about himself.

June 25

*E*ver to be remembered is that best and brightest of hours when we first saw the Lord, lost our burden, received the roll of promise, rejoiced in full salvation, and went on our way in peace. It was springtime in the soul; the winter was past. Then the flowers appeared in our heart. Hope, love, peace, and patience sprang from the sod, and our resolve was, "Lord, I am Yours, wholly Yours; all I am, and all I have, I would devote to You. You have bought me with Your blood; let me spend myself and be spent in Your service. In life and in death let me be consecrated to You."

How have we kept this resolve?

June 26

When thou shalt make his soul an offering for sin, he shall see his seed.—Isaiah 53:10

*O*ur Lord Jesus has not died in vain. His death was sacrificial; He died as our substitute because death was the penalty of our sins and because His substitution was accepted by God. He has saved those for whom He made His soul a sacrifice. By death He became like the corn of wheat which brings forth much fruit. There must be a succession of children to Jesus; He is the Father of the everlasting age. He will say, "Behold I and the children which God hath given me" (Heb. 2:13).

June 27

*M*y own sight of the precious blood is for my comfort, but it is the Lord's sight of it which secures my safety. Even when I am unable to behold it, the Lord looks at it and passes over me because of it. None can tell His delight in Jesus. Now we rest in calm security. We have God's sacrifice and God's Word to create in us a sense of perfect security. He will, He must, pass over us because He did not spare our glorious Substitute. Justice joins hands with love to provide everlasting salvation for all the blood-sprinkled ones.

June 28

*T*he branch is not only ever near the stem but ever receiving life and fruitfulness from it. All true believers abide in Christ in a sense, but there is a higher meaning. This we must know before we gain unlimited power at the throne. "Ask what ye will" (John 15:7) is for Enochs who walk with God, for Johns who lie in the Lord's bosom, for those whose union with Christ leads to constant communion.

If you would be mighty in your pleadings, the Lord Himself must abide in you and you in Him.

June 29

Be careful for nothing; but in every thing by prayer and supplication with thanksgiving let your requests be made known unto God. And the peace of God, which passeth all understanding, shall keep your hearts and minds through Christ Jesus.—Philippians 4:6–7

*N*o care but all prayer. No anxiety but much joyful communion with God. Carry your desires to the Lord of your life, the guardian of your soul. Go to Him with two portions of prayer and one of fragrant praise. Do not pray doubtfully but thankfully. Consider that you have your petitions, and, therefore, thank God for His grace.

June 30

When a man's ways please the LORD, he maketh even his enemies to be at peace with him.—Proverbs 16:7

I must see that my ways please the Lord. Even then I will have enemies, and perhaps all the more certainly because I endeavored to do that which is right. But what a promise this is! The Lord will make the wrath of men to praise Him and abate it so that it will not distress me. When I meet death, who is called "the last enemy" (1 Cor. 15:26), I pray that I may be at peace. Only let my great care be to please the Lord in all things.

July 1

R eturn unto the LORD thy God" (Hos. 14:1). Where we first found salvation, we will find it again—at the foot of Christ's cross, confessing sin. Moreover, the Lord will have us obey His voice according to all that He has commanded us. We must do this with all our hearts and all our souls, and then our captivity will end.

Often depression of spirit and great misery of soul are removed as soon as we quit our idols and bow ourselves to obedience before the living God. We may return to Zion's citizenship, and that speedily. Lord, turn our captivity!

July 2

F riendship, though very pleasing and exceedingly blessed, has been the cause of the greatest misery to men when it has been unworthy and unfaithful. Just in proportion as a good friend is sweet, a false friend is full of bitterness. A faithless friend is sharper than an adder's tooth. It is sweet to repose in someone, but how bitter it is to have that support snapped and to receive a grievous fall as the effect of your confidence. Solomon declares that "there is a friend that sticketh closer than a brother" (Prov. 18:24). That friend, I suppose, he never found in the pomp and vanities of the world. He had tried them all, but he found them empty; he passed through all their joys.

July 3

*C*ould faith believe in a being more answerable to all our needs, more helpful to our noblest longings? Allied to Jesus, we confidently aspire to such likeness to our Creator as is possible for a creature to bear. Nor is the advantage less in the other direction, for here is a man, bound to us by the most intense relationship and affection, who is not only tender to the last degree of our suffering nature but is also as wise as He is brotherly and as mighty to subdue our faults as He is gentle to bear with our frailties. His manhood brings Jesus down to us, but united with the divine nature, it lifts us up to God. The Lord Jesus, thus, not only ministers to our comfort but to our betterment, the greater concern.

July 4

*A*ll they that heard it wondered at those things" (Luke 2:18). We must not cease to wonder at the great marvels of our God. It would be very difficult to draw a line between holy wonder and real worship, for when the soul is overwhelmed with the majesty of God's glory, though it may not express itself in song or even utter its voice with bowed head and humble prayer, it silently adores. Our incarnate God is to be worshipped as "the Wonderful." That God should consider His fallen creature, man, and should Himself undertake to be man's Redeemer and to pay his ransom price is, indeed, marvelous!

July 5

*C*hrist will be master of the heart, and sin must be mortified. If your life is unholy, your heart is unchanged; you are an unsaved person. If the Savior has not sanctified you, renewed you, given you a hatred of sin and a love of holiness, the grace which does not make a man better than others is a worthless counterfeit. Christ saves His people, not in their sins but from them. Without holiness "no man shall see the Lord" (Heb. 12:14). "Let every one that nameth the name of Christ depart from iniquity" (2 Tim. 2:19). If not saved from sin, how can we hope to be counted among His people? Lord, save me even now from all evil, and enable me to honor my Savior.

July 6

*E*very branch that beareth fruit, he purgeth it, that it may bring forth more fruit" (John 15:2). If you bring forth fruit, you will have to endure affliction. But this affliction works out such precious results that the Christian who is the subject of it must learn to rejoice in tribulations, because as his tribulations abound so his consolations abound because of Christ Jesus. Rest assured, if you are a child of God, you will be no stranger to the rod. Sooner or later every bar of gold must pass through the fire. You will be delivered from clinging to the present and made to long for those eternal things which are so soon to be revealed to you.

July 7

God ordains with accurate wisdom the most fitting time for the redeemed to abide below. Surely, if there could be regrets in heaven, the saints might mourn that they did not live longer here to do more good. Oh, for more sheaves for my Lord's harvest! More jewels for His crown! But how, unless there is more work? When we are fully serving God, and He is giving us to scatter precious seed and reap a hundredfold, we would even say it is well for us to abide where we are. Whether our Master will say "go," or "stay," let us be equally well pleased, so long as He indulges us with His presence.

July 8

As an encouragement to offer intercessory prayer cheerfully, remember that such prayer is the sweetest God ever hears, for the prayer of Christ is of this character. His intercession must be the most acceptable of all supplications, and the more like our prayer is to Christ's, the sweeter it will be. Thus, while petitions for ourselves will be accepted, our pleadings for others, having in them more of the fruits of the Spirit—more love, more faith, more brotherly kindness—will be, through the precious merits of Jesus, the sweetest offering that we can offer to God, the very fat of our sacrifice. Remember, again, that intercessory prayer is exceedingly prevalent. What wonders it has wrought!

July 9

*I*t is true I am weak in faith and prone to fall, but my very feebleness is the reason why I should always be where He feeds His flock that I may be strengthened and preserved in safety beside the still waters. Why should I turn aside? There is no reason why I should, but there are a thousand reasons why I should not, for Jesus beckons me to come. If He withdraws Himself a little, it is but to make me prize His presence more. Now that I am grieved and distressed at being away from Him, He will lead me yet again to that sheltered nook where the lambs of His fold are sheltered from the burning sun.

July 10

*W*ithout Him we can do nothing (see John 15:5), but by His almighty energy the most extraordinary results can be produced. Everything depends upon His manifesting or concealing His power. Do we always look up to Him, both for our inner life and our outward service, with the respectful dependence which is fitting? Do we not too often run before His call and act independently of His aid? Let us humble ourselves this day for past neglects and now entreat the heavenly dew to rest upon us, the sacred oil to anoint us, the celestial flame to burn within us. The Holy Spirit is no temporary gift; He abides with the saints. We have but to seek Him aright, and He will be found by us.

*T*he sovereign choice of the Father, by which He elected us unto eternal life, is a matter of vast antiquity since no date can be conceived for it by the mind of man. We were chosen from before the foundations of the world. (See Ephesians 1:4.) Everlasting love went with the choice. It was not a bare act of divine will by which we were set apart, but the divine affections were concerned. The Father loved us in and from the beginning. Here is a theme for daily contemplation. The eternal purpose to redeem us from our foreseen ruin, to cleanse and sanctify us, and at last to glorify us, was of infinite antiquity and runs side by side with immutable love and absolute sovereignty.

July 12

*W*e have not so clear a view of Him as we could wish. We know not the heights and depths of His love, but we know of a surety that He is too good to withdraw from a trembling soul the gift which it has been able to obtain. If we "have faith as a grain of mustard seed" (Matt. 17:20), salvation is our present and eternal possession. If we cannot clasp the Lord in our hands with Simeon, if we dare not lean our heads upon His bosom with John, yet if we can venture in the press behind Him and touch the hem of His garment, we are made whole. Courage, timid one! "Thy faith hath saved thee; go in peace" (Luke 7:50). "Being justified by faith, we have peace with God" (Rom. 5:1).

July 13

*W*hereby they have made thee glad" (Ps. 45:8). And who are thus privileged to make the Savior glad? His church—His people. But is it possible? He makes us glad, but how can we make Him glad? By our love. See, loving heart, how He delights in you. When you lean your head on His bosom, you not only receive, but you give Him joy; when you gaze with love upon His all-glorious face, you not only obtain comfort but impart delight. Our praise, too, gives Him joy—not the song of the lips alone but the melody of the heart's deep gratitude. He loves us, not for the value of what we give but for the motive from which the gift springs.

July 14

*I*f the Lord is with us through life, we need not fear for our dying confidence, for when we come to die, we will find that "The LORD is there" (Ezek. 48:35). Where the billows are most tempestuous and the water is most chill, we will feel the bottom and know that it is good; our feet will stand upon the Rock of Ages when time is passing away. Beloved, from the first of a Christian's life to the last, the only reason why he does not perish is because "the LORD is there." When the God of everlasting love will change and leave His elect to perish, then may the church of God be destroyed, but not until then because it is written, Jehovah, "The LORD is there."

July 15

Common, too common, is the sin of forgetting the Holy Spirit. This is folly and ingratitude. He deserves honor at our hands, for He is good, supremely good. As God, He is good essentially. He shares in the threefold ascription of "Holy, holy, holy" (Isa. 6:3), which ascends to the triune Jehovah. Unmixed purity and truth and grace is He. He is good benevolently, tenderly bearing with our waywardness, striving with our rebellious wills, quickening us from our death in sin, and then training us for the skies as a loving nurse fosters her child. How generous, forgiving, and tender is this patient Spirit of God.

July 16

He first findeth his own brother Simon" (John 1:41). Let your religion begin at home; take care to put forth the sweetest fruit of spiritual life and testimony in your own family. You may be very deficient in talent yourself, and yet you may be the means of drawing to Christ one who will become eminent in grace and service. Ah, dear friend, you little know the possibilities which are in you. You may but speak a word to a child, and in that child there may be slumbering a noble heart which will stir the Christian church in years to come. Andrew had only two talents, but he found Peter. "Go, and do thou likewise" (Luke 10:37).

July 17

*I*t is quite certain that those whom Christ has washed in His precious blood need not make a confession of sin as culprits or criminals before God the Judge, for Christ has forever taken away all their sins so that they no longer stand where they can be condemned. However, having become children, and offending as children, ought they not every day to go before their heavenly Father and confess their sin and acknowledge their iniquity? Nature teaches that it is the duty of erring children to make a confession to their earthly father, and the grace of God in the heart teaches us that we, as Christians, owe the same duty to our heavenly Father.

July 18

*W*e would be abler teachers of others, and less liable to be carried about by every wind of doctrine, if we sought to have a more intelligent understanding of the Word of God. As the Holy Spirit, the Author of the Scriptures, is the only Teacher who can enlighten us rightly to understand them, we should constantly ask His teaching and His guidance "into all truth" (John 16:13).

Therefore if, for your own and others' profiting, you desire to "be filled with the knowledge of [God's] will in all wisdom and spiritual understanding" (Col. 1:9), remember that prayer is your best means of study. You may force your way through anything with the leverage of prayer.

*T*he LORD is slow to anger, and great in power" (Nah. 1:3), but the greatness of His power brings us mercy. Dear reader, what is your state this day? Can you by humble faith look to Jesus and say, "My substitute, You are my rock, my trust"? Then, beloved, be not afraid of God's power, for now that you are forgiven and accepted, now that by faith you have fled to Christ for refuge, the power of God need no more terrify you than the shield and sword of the warrior need terrify those whom he loves. Rather rejoice that He who is "great in power" is your Father and Friend.

July 20

*Y*ou have not the making of your own cross. Your cross is prepared and appointed for you by divine love, and you are to accept it cheerfully. This day Jesus bids you to submit your shoulder to His easy yoke. Jesus was a cross-bearer; He leads the way in the path of sorrow. Surely you could not desire a better guide! And if He carries a cross, what nobler burden would you desire? The *Via Crucis* is the way of safety; fear not to tread its thorny paths.

It is a wooden cross, and a man can carry it, for the Man of Sorrows tried the load. Take up your cross, and by the power of the Spirit of God you will soon love it.

July 21

*T*here are occasions when God's servants shrink from duty. But what is the consequence? They lose the presence and comfortable enjoyment of God's love. When we obey our Lord Jesus as believers should, our God is with us, and though we have the whole world against us, if we have God with us, what does it matter? But the moment we start back and seek our own inventions, we are at sea without a pilot. Then may we bitterly lament and groan out, "Oh, my God, where have You gone? How could I have been so foolish as to lose the bright shining of Your face? This is a price too high. Let me return to my allegiance, that I may rejoice in Your presence."

July 22

*W*hen God seems most to leave His church, His heart is warm towards her. History shows us that whenever God uses a rod to chasten His servants, He always breaks it afterwards, as if He loathed the rod which gave His children pain. "Like as a father pitieth his children, so the LORD pitieth them that fear him" (Ps. 103:13). His blows are no evidences of want of love. You may fear that the Lord has passed you by, but it is not so. He who counts the stars and calls them by their names (Ps. 147:4) is in no danger of forgetting His own children. He knows your case as thoroughly as if you were the only creature He ever made or the only saint He ever loved. Approach Him, and be at peace.

*T*hose "goings forth have been from of old, from everlasting" (Mic. 5:2). The Lord Jesus had goings forth for His people, as their representative before the throne, long before they appeared upon the stage of time. It was "from everlasting" that He signed the compact with His Father that He would pay blood for blood, suffering for suffering, agony for agony, and death for death on the behalf of His people. It was "from everlasting" that He gave Himself up without a murmuring word. His "goings forth" as our surety were "from everlasting." Pause, my soul, and wonder! You had goings forth in the person of Jesus "from everlasting."

July 24

*N*ot only when you were born into the world did Christ love you, but His delights were with the sons of men before there were any sons of men. Often did He think of them; from everlasting to everlasting He had set His affections upon them. (See Jeremiah 31:3.) I am sure He would not have loved me for so long if He had not been a changeless lover. If He could grow weary of me, He would have been tired of me long before now. If He had not loved me with a love as deep as life and as strong as death, He would have turned from me long ago. Oh, joy above all joys, to know that I am His everlasting and inalienable inheritance, given to Him by His Father.

*M*ight not Jesus well say to us, "I have some-what against thee, because thou hast left thy first love" (Rev. 2:4). Alas! It is but little we have done for our Master's glory. Our winter has lasted all too long. We give to God pence when He deserves pounds—nay, deserves our heart's blood to be coined in the service of His church and of His truth. But will we continue this? O Lord, after You have so richly blessed us, will we be ungrateful and become indifferent to Your good cause and work? Oh, quicken us that we may return to our first love and do our first works! Send us a genial spring, Sun of Righteousness.

*B*lessed Lord Jesus, be with me, reveal Yourself, and abide with me all night, so that when I awake, I may be with You still. I note that the dove brought in her mouth an olive branch plucked off, the memorial of the past and a prophecy of the future. Have I no pleasing record to bring home? No pledge and earnest of loving-kindness yet to come? Yes, my Lord, I present to You my grateful acknowledgments for tender mercies which have been new every morning and fresh every evening (Lam. 3:22–23). Now, I pray, put forth Your hand, and take Your dove into Your bosom.

July 27

*A*s the Spirit of God descended upon the Lord Jesus, the Head, so He also, in measure, descends upon the members of the mystical body. His descent is to us after the same fashion as that in which it fell upon our Lord. There is often a singular rapidity about it, and as we become aware, we are impelled onward and heavenward beyond all expectation. The brooding of the Spirit of God upon the face of the deep first produced order and life, and in our hearts He causes and fosters new life and light. Blessed Spirit, as You did rest upon our dear Redeemer, even so rest upon us from this time forward and forever.

July 28

The barrel of meal wasted not, neither did the cruse of oil fail, according to the word of the LORD, which he spake by Elijah.—1 Kings 17:16

*Y*ou, dear reader, have daily necessities, and because they come so frequently, you are apt to fear that the barrel of meal will one day be empty and the cruse of oil will fail you. (See 1 Kings 17:14.) Rest assured that, according to the Word of God, this will not be the case. Each day, though it bring its trouble, will bring its help. Though you should live to outnumber the years of Methuselah and though your needs should be as many as the sands of the seashore, God's grace and mercy will last through all your necessities, and you will never know a real lack.

July 29

*W*ords cannot set forth the preciousness of the Lord Jesus to His people. Dear reader, what would you do in the world without Him in the midst of its temptations and its cares? What would you do in the morning without Him when you wake up and look forward to the day's battle? What would you do at night when you come home jaded and weary if there were no door of fellowship between you and Christ? Blessed be His name, He will not suffer us to try our lot without Him, for Jesus never forsakes His own. Yet, let the thought of what life would be without Him enhance his preciousness.

July 30

*B*e not content with an interview now and then, but seek always to retain His company, for only in His presence do you have either comfort or safety. Jesus should not be to us a friend who calls upon us now and then but one with whom we walk evermore. You have a difficult road before you; see, traveler to heaven, that you do not go without your guide. You have to pass through the fiery furnace; enter it not unless, like Shadrach, Meshach, and Abednego, you have the Son of God to be your companion. In every condition you will need Jesus. Keep close to your best Friend, and He will refresh and cheer you.

*T*here is a time appointed for weakness and sickness when we will have to glorify God by suffering and not by earnest activity. There is no single point in which we can hope to escape from the sharp arrows of affliction. Out of our few days there is not one secure from sorrow. Beloved reader, do not set your affections upon things of earth, but seek those things which are above. *Here* the moth devours and the thief breaks through, but *there* all joys are perpetual and eternal. The path of trouble is the way home. Lord, make this thought a pillow for many a weary head!

August 1

*C*ommunion with Christ is a certain cure for every ill. Whether it is the bitterness of woe or the cloying excess of earthly delight, close fellowship with the Lord Jesus will take bitterness from the one and fullness from the other. Live near to Jesus, Christian, and it is matter of secondary importance whether you live on the mountain of honor or in the valley of humiliation. Living near to Jesus, you are covered with the wings of God, and underneath you are the everlasting arms. Let nothing keep you from that hallowed intercourse which is the choice privilege of a soul wedded to the Well Beloved.

August 2

*D*oubtless, the reader has been tried with the temptation to rely upon things which are seen instead of resting alone upon the invisible God. Christians often look to man for help and counsel and mar the noble simplicity of their reliance upon their God. Does this portion meet the eye of a child of God anxious about temporal things? Then we would reason with him a while. You trust in Jesus, and only in Jesus, for your salvation, so why are you troubled? "Because of my great care." Is it not written, "Cast thy burden upon the LORD" (Ps. 55:22)? "Be careful for nothing; but in every thing by prayer and supplication...let your requests be made known unto God" (Phil. 4:6).

August 3

*T*hough the host that feeds at Jehovah's table is as countless as the stars of heaven, yet each one has his portion of meat. Think how much grace one saint requires, so much that nothing but the Infinite could supply him for one day. Yet the Lord spreads His table, not for one but for many saints, not for one day but for many years. The guests at mercy's banquet are satisfied—nay, more "abundantly satisfied" (Ps. 36:8)—not with ordinary fare but with fatness, the peculiar fatness of God's own house. Such feasting is guaranteed by a faithful promise to all those children of men who put their trust under the shadow of Jehovah's wings.

August 4

*T*his is no unusual occurrence; it is the general rule of the moral universe that those men who do their work with all their hearts prosper, while those who go to their labor leaving half their hearts behind them are almost certain to fail. God does not give harvests to idle men, except harvests of thistles, nor is He pleased to send wealth to those who will not dig in the field to find its hidden treasure. It is universally confessed that if man would prosper, he must be diligent in business.

It is the same in religion as it is in other things. If you would prosper in your work for Jesus, let it be heart work, and let it be done with all your heart.

August 5

How constantly our Master used the title, the "Son of Man!" If He had chosen, He might always have spoken of Himself as the Son of God, the Everlasting Father, the Wonderful, the Counselor, the Prince of Peace; but behold the lowliness of Jesus! He prefers to call himself the Son of Man. Let us learn a lesson of humility from our Savior. Jesus loved manhood so much that He delighted to honor it. Since it is a high honor—indeed, the greatest dignity of manhood—that Jesus is the Son of Man, He is accustomed to display this name that He may, as it were, hang royal stars upon the breast of manhood and show forth the love of God to Abraham's seed.

August 6

Whenever we are privileged to eat of the bread which Jesus gives, we are satisfied with the full and sweet repast. When Jesus is the host, no guest goes empty from the table. Our heads are satisfied with the precious truth which Christ reveals. Our hearts are content with Jesus. Our hopes are satisfied, for whom have we in heaven but Jesus? And, our desires are satiated, for what can we wish for more than to know Christ and to be found in Him? Jesus fills our consciences until they are at perfect peace, our judgments with the certainty of His teachings, our memories with recollections of what He has done, and our imaginations with the prospects of what He is yet to do.

August 7

*T*wo opinions in the matter of soul-religion you cannot hold. If God is God, serve Him, and do it thoroughly. However, if this world is God, serve it, and make no profession of religion. If you think the things of the world the best, serve them. But remember, if the Lord is your God, you cannot have Baal, too; you must have one thing or else the other. "No man can serve two masters" (Matt. 6:24). If God is served, He will be a master. If the devil is served, it will not be long before he will be a master, and "no man can serve two masters." Oh! Be wise, and think not that the two can be mingled together.

August 8

*T*he Savior was "a man of sorrows" (Isa. 53:3), but every thoughtful mind has discovered the fact that down deep in His innermost soul He carried an inexhaustible treasury of refined and heavenly joy. Of all the human race, there was never a man who had a deeper, purer, or more abiding peace than our Lord Jesus Christ. He was anointed "with the oil of gladness above [His] fellows" (Heb. 1:9). His vast benevolence must have afforded Him the deepest possible delight, for benevolence is joy. There were a few remarkable seasons when this joy manifested itself. "In that hour Jesus rejoiced in spirit, and said, I thank thee, O Father, Lord of heaven and earth" (Luke 10:21).

August 9

*H*old thou me up, and I shall be safe" (Ps. 119:117). Having prayed, you must also watch, guarding every thought, word, and action with holy jealousy. Do not expose yourself unnecessarily, but if called to exposure, if you are bidden to go where the darts are flying, never venture forth without your shield, for the devil will rejoice that his hour of triumph is come and will soon make you fall down wounded by his arrows. Though you cannot be slain, you may be wounded. "Be sober, be vigilant" (1 Pet. 5:8); danger may be in an hour when all seems secure to you. Therefore, take heed to your ways, and watch unto prayer. May the Holy Spirit guide us in all our ways.

August 10

*S*on of Man—whenever He said that word, He shed a halo round the head of Adam's children. Jesus Christ called Himself the Son of Man to express His oneness and sympathy with His people. He thus reminds us that He is one whom we may approach without fear. As a man, we may take to Him all our griefs and troubles, for He knows them by experience. In that He Himself has suffered as the Son of Man, He is able to succor and comfort us.

All hail, blessed Jesus! Inasmuch as You are evermore using the sweet name which acknowledges that You are a brother and a near kinsman, it is to us a dear token of Your grace, Your humility, and Your love.

August 11

Wholeheartedness shows itself in perseverance. There may be failure at first, but the earnest worker will say, "It is the Lord's work, and it must be done. My Lord has bidden me to do it, and in His strength I will accomplish it." Christian, are you thus with all your heart serving your Master? Remember the earnestness of Jesus! Think what heart-work was His! He could say, "The zeal of thine house hath eaten me up" (Ps. 69:9). When He sweat great drops of blood, it was no light burden He had to carry upon those blessed shoulders, and when He poured out His heart, it was no weak effort He was making for the salvation of His people.

August 12

Whether we speak of the active or passive righteousness of Christ, there is an equal fragrance. There was a sweet savor in His active life by which He honored the law of God and made every precept to glitter like a precious jewel in the pure setting of His own person. Such, too, was His passive obedience when He endured, with unmurmuring submission, hunger and thirst, cold and nakedness, and at length was fastened to the cruel cross that He might suffer the wrath of God on our behalf. These two things are sweet before the Most High, and for the sake of His doing and His dying, His substitutionary sufferings, and His vicarious obedience, the Lord our God accepts us.

August 13

*A*s the Father loves the Son, in the same manner Jesus loves His people. He loved Him without beginning, and thus Jesus loves us. "I have loved thee with an everlasting love" (Jer. 31:3). You can trace the beginning of human affection; you can easily find the beginning of your love to Christ, but His love to us is a stream whose source is hidden in eternity. God the Father loves Jesus without any change. Christian, take this for your comfort: there is no change in Jesus Christ's love to those who rest in Him. Yesterday you were on the mount, and you said, "He loves me"; today you are in the valley of humiliation, but He loves you still the same.

August 14

And she said, Truth, Lord: yet the dogs eat of the crumbs which fall from their masters' table.—Matthew 15:27

*M*y sins are many, but, oh, it is nothing to Jesus to take them all away. "It will be but a small thing for Him to give me full remission, although it will be an infinite blessing for me to receive it." The woman opens her soul wide, expecting great things of Jesus, and He fills it with His love. Dear reader, do the same. She laid fast hold upon Him, drew arguments even out of His words. She believed great things of Him, and she thus overcame Him. She won the victory by believing in Him. Her case is an instance of prevailing faith, and if we would conquer like her, we must imitate her.

August 15

*T*o whom belongest thou?" (1 Sam. 30:13). Let me assist you, reader, in your response. Have you been "born again"? If you have, you belong to Christ, but without the new birth you cannot be His. In whom do you trust? Those who believe in Jesus are the sons of God. Whose work are you doing? You are sure to serve your master, for he whom you serve is thereby owned to be your lord. What is your conversation? Is it heavenly, or is it earthly? What have you learned of your master? If you have served your time with Jesus, it will be said of you, as it was of Peter and John, "They took knowledge of them, that they had been with Jesus" (Acts 4:13).

August 16

*T*he lives of some of God's people fill us with holy astonishment. Strange and marvelous are the ways which God used in their cases to find His own. Blessed be His name, He never relinquishes the search until the chosen are sought out effectually. They are not a people sought today and cast away tomorrow. Almightiness and wisdom combined will make no failures. They will be called "Sought out" (Isa. 62:12). That any should be sought out is matchless grace, but that we should be sought out is grace beyond degree! We can find no reason for it but God's own sovereign love and can only lift up our hearts in wonder and praise the Lord that this day we wear the name of "Sought out."

*W*e have sat at the table of the Lord's love and said, "Nothing but the infinite can satisfy me. I am such a great sinner that I must have infinite merit to wash my sin away," but we have had our sin removed and found that there was merit to spare. We have had our hunger relieved at the feast of sacred love and found that there was an abundance of spiritual meat remaining. Yes, there are graces to which we have not attained, places of fellowship nearer to Christ which we have not reached, and heights of communion which our feet have not climbed. At every banquet of love there are many baskets of fragments left. Let us magnify the liberality of our glorious Redeemer.

*W*earied out with her wanderings, the dove returns at length to the ark as her only resting place. Noah has been looking out for his dove all day long and is ready to receive her. She has just strength to reach the edge of the ark when Noah puts forth his hand and pulls her in to him. She did not fly right in herself but was too fearful, or too weary, to do so. She flew as far as she could, and then he put forth his hand and pulled her in to him. Just as she was, she was pulled into the ark. So you, seeking sinner, with all your sin, will be received. Only return—these are God's two gracious words— "only return."

August 19

*A*t this hour the church expects to walk in sympathy with her Lord along a thorny road. Through much tribulation, she is forcing her way to the crown. To bear the cross is her office, and yet the church has a deep well of joy of which none can drink but her own children. There are stores of wine and oil and corn hidden in the midst of our Jerusalem upon which the saints of God are evermore sustained and nurtured. Sometimes, as in our Savior's case, we have our seasons of intense delight, for "There is a river, the streams whereof shall make glad the city of God" (Ps. 46:4). Exiles though we are, we rejoice in our King; yes, in Him we exceedingly rejoice.

August 20

*T*he Father loves the Son *without any end*, and thus does the Son love His people. Rest confident that, even down to the grave, Christ will go with you and that, up again from it, He will be your guide to the celestial hills. Moreover, the Father loves the Son *without any measure*, and the Son bestows the same immeasurable love upon His chosen ones. The whole heart of Christ is dedicated to His people. He "loved us, and hath given himself for us" (Eph. 5:2). His is a love which passes knowledge. Ah, we have indeed a precious Savior, one who loves without measure, without change, without beginning, without end, even as the Father loves Him!

A little stay on earth will make heaven more heavenly. Nothing makes rest so sweet as toil. Our battered armor and scarred countenances will render our victory above more illustrious, when we are welcomed to the seats of those who have overcome the world. We should not have full fellowship with Christ if we did not for a while sojourn below, for He was baptized with a baptism of suffering among men, and we must be baptized with the same if we would share His kingdom. Fellowship with Christ is so honorable that the sorest sorrow is a light price by which to procure it.

August 22

D ivine omniscience affords no comfort to the ungodly mind, but to the child of God it overflows with consolation. God is always thinking upon us and never turns His mind aside from us, for it would be dreadful to exist for a moment beyond the observation of our heavenly Father. His thoughts are always tender, loving, and far-reaching, and they bring to us countless benefits. The Lord always did think upon His people, hence their election and the covenant of grace by which their salvation is secured. He always will think upon them, hence their final perseverance by which they will be brought safely to their final rest.

*I*f trained by the Great Teacher, we follow where He leads. We will find good even while in this dark abode. But where will this wisdom be found? Many have dreamed of it but have not possessed it. Where will we learn it? Let us listen to the voice of the Lord, for he has declared the secret. He has revealed to the sons of men wherein true wisdom lies, and we have in it the text, "Whoso trusteth in the LORD, happy is he" (Prov. 16:20). The true way to handle a matter wisely is to trust in the Lord. This is the sure clue to the most intricate labyrinths of life.

Lord, in this sweet eventide, walk with me in the garden and teach me the wisdom of faith.

*I*t is well for us when prayers about our sorrows are linked with pleas concerning our sins, when, being under God's hand, we are not wholly taken up with our pain but remember our offenses against God. It is well also to take both sorrow and sin to the same place. It was to God that David carried his sorrow; it was to God that David confessed his sin. Observe, then, we must take our sorrows to God. Even your little sorrows you may roll upon God, for He counts the hairs of your head, and your great sorrows you may commit to Him, for He holds the ocean in the hollow of His hand.

August 25

*P*rayer sometimes tarries like a petitioner at the gate until the King comes forth to fill her bosom with the blessings which she seeks. The Lord, when he has given great faith, has been known to try it by long delayings. He has suffered his servants' voices to echo in their ears as from a brazen sky. Unanswered petitions are not unheard. By and by your suit will prevail. Can you not be content to wait a little? Will not your Lord's time be better than your time? By and by He will comfortably appear, to your soul's joy, and make you put away the sackcloth and ashes of long waiting and put on the scarlet and fine linen of full fruition.

August 26

*I*n all our wanderings, the watchful glance of the Eternal Watcher is evermore fixed upon us—we never roam beyond the Shepherd's eye. In our sorrows, He observes us incessantly, and not a pang escapes Him. In our toils, He marks all our weariness and writes in His book all the struggles of His faithful ones. These thoughts of the Lord encompass us in all our paths and penetrate the innermost region of our being.

Dear reader, is this precious to you? Then hold to it. The Lord lives and thinks upon us; this is a truth far too precious for us to be lightly robbed of it. If the Lord thinks upon us, all is well, and we may rejoice evermore.

*B*ehold the epitaph of all those blessed saints who fell asleep before the coming of our Lord! It matters nothing how else they died, and this one point, in which they all agree, is the most worthy of record: "These all died in faith" (Heb. 11:13). In faith they lived. It was their comfort, their guide, their motive, and their support, and in the same spiritual grace they died, ending their life-song in the sweet strain in which they had so long continued. They did not die resting in the flesh or upon their own achievements; they made no advance from their first way of acceptance with God but held to the way of faith to the end.

August 28

*W*e are so little that if God should manifest His greatness without condescension, we should be trampled under His feet. But God, who must stoop to view the skies and bow to see what angels do, turns His eye yet lower and looks to the lowly and contrite and makes them great.

"Thy gentleness hath made me great" (2 Sam. 22:36). How marvelous has been our experience of God's gentleness! How gentle have been His corrections! How gentle His teachings! How gentle His drawings! Meditate upon this theme, believer. Let gratitude be awakened; let humility be deepened; let love be quickened before this day closes.

*H*ow independent of outward circumstances the Holy Spirit can make the Christian! What a bright light may shine within us when it is all dark without! How firm, how happy, how calm, how peaceful we may be when the world shakes to and fro and the pillars of the earth are removed! Even death itself, with all its terrible influences, has no power to suspend the music of a Christian's heart. Rather it makes that music become more sweet, more clear, more heavenly, until the last kind act which death can do is to let the earthly strain melt into the heavenly chorus, the temporal joy into the eternal bliss!

August 30

*O*ur Lord Jesus, by His death, did not purchase a right to a part of us only but to the entire man. He contemplated in His passion the sanctification of us wholly: spirit, soul, and body. It is the business of the new-born nature which God has given to the regenerate heart to assert the rights of the Lord Jesus Christ. My soul, so far as you are a child of God, you must conquer all the rest of yourself which yet remains unblessed. You must subdue all your powers and passions to the silver scepter of Jesus' gracious reign, and you must never be satisfied until He who is king by purchase also becomes king by gracious coronation and reigns in you supreme.

*W*isdom is man's true strength, and under its guidance, he best accomplishes the ends of his being. Wisely handling the matters of life gives to man the richest enjoyment and presents the noblest occupation for his powers; therefore, by it, he finds good in the fullest sense. Without wisdom, man is as the wild ass's colt, running hither and thither, wasting strength which might be profitably employed. Wisdom is the compass by which man is to steer across the trackless waste of life; without it he is a derelict vessel, the sport of winds and waves. A man must be prudent in such a world as this, or he will find no good but be betrayed into unnumbered ills.

September 1

*I*t is easy work to pray when we are grounded, as to our desires, upon God's own promise. How can He that gave the word refuse to keep it? Immutable veracity cannot demean itself by a lie, and eternal faithfulness cannot degrade itself by neglect. God must bless His Son; His covenant binds Him to it. That which the Spirit prompts us to ask of God for Jesus and His kingdom is that which God decrees to give Him. Whenever you are praying for the kingdom of Christ, let your eyes behold the dawning of the blessed day, which draws near, when the Crucified will receive His coronation in the place where men rejected Him.

September 2

*I*f we fear the Lord, we may look for timely interpositions when our case is at its worst. Angels are not kept from us by storms or hindered by darkness. Seraphs think it no humiliation to visit the poorest of the heavenly family. If angels' visits are few and far between at ordinary times, they will be frequent in our nights of tempest and tossing.

Dear reader, is this an hour of distress with you? Then ask for peculiar help. Jesus is the angel of the covenant, and if His presence is now earnestly sought, it will not be denied. What that presence brings is heart cheer.

September 3

*D*ying in faith has distinct reference to the past. Saints of old believed the promises which had gone before and were assured that their sins were blotted out through the mercy of God. Dying in faith has to do with the present. These saints were confident of their acceptance with God; they enjoyed the beams of His love and rested in His faithfulness. Dying in faith looks into the future. They fell asleep, affirming that the Messiah would surely come. Your course, through grace, is one of faith, and sight seldom cheers you; this has also been the pathway of the brightest and the best.

September 4

*I*t is exceedingly beneficial to our souls to mount above this present evil world to something nobler and better. It would be well if the dwellers in the valley could frequently leave their abodes among the marshes and the fever mists and inhale the bracing element upon the hills. It is to such an exploit of climbing that I now invite you. May the Spirit of God assist us to leave the mists of fear and the fevers of anxiety and all the ills which gather in this valley of earth and to ascend the mountains of anticipated joy and blessedness. May God the Holy Spirit cut the cords that keep us here below and assist us to mount.

September 5

*B*e courageous concerning this, Christian! Be not dispirited, as though your spiritual enemies could never be destroyed; you are Christ's, and sin has no right to you.

You are able to overcome them, not in your own strength—the weakest of them would be too much for you in that—but you can and will overcome them through the blood of the Lamb. Do not ask, "How will I dispossess them, for they are greater and mightier than I?" Go to the strong for strength, wait humbly upon God, and the mighty God of Jacob will surely come to the rescue. Then you will sing of victory through His grace.

September 6

*T*o this man will I look, even to him that is poor and of a contrite spirit, and trembleth at my word" (Isa. 66:2). Stoop if you would climb to heaven. Do we not say of Jesus that He descended so that He might ascend? (See Ephesians 4:9–10.) So must you. You must grow downwards that you may grow upwards, for the sweetest fellowship with heaven is to be had by humble souls, and by them alone. God will deny no blessing to a thoroughly humbled spirit. Humility makes us ready to be blessed by the God of all grace and fits us to deal efficiently with our fellowmen. Whether it is prayer or praise, whether it is work or suffering, the genuine salt of humility cannot be used in excess.

September 7

*H*allowed be thy name. Thy kingdom come. Thy will be done in earth, as it is in heaven" (Matt. 6:9–10). Let not your prayers be all concerning your own sins, your own wants, your own imperfections, and your own trials, but let them climb the starry ladder and get up to Christ Himself. Then, as you draw nigh to the blood-sprinkled mercy seat, offer this prayer continually, "Lord, extend the kingdom of Your dear Son." Such a petition, fervently presented, will elevate the spirit of all your devotions. Mind that you prove the sincerity of your prayer by laboring to promote the Lord's glory.

September 8

*S*earch the scriptures" (John 5:39). The Greek word here rendered *search* signifies a strict, close, diligent search, such as men make when they are seeking gold or hunters when they are in earnest after game. We must not rest content with having given a superficial reading to a chapter or two, but with the candle of the Spirit, we must deliberately seek out the hidden meaning of the Word. Holy Scripture requires searching—much of it can only be learned by careful study. No man who merely skims the Book of God can profit thereby; we must dig and mine until we obtain the hidden treasure. The Scriptures claim searching.

September 9

*T*he LORD is my light and my salvation" (Ps. 27:1). Here is personal interest: "my light," "my salvation." The soul is assured of it and, therefore, declares it boldly. Into the soul at the new birth, divine light is poured as the precursor of salvation. Where there is not enough light to reveal our own darkness and to make us long for the Lord Jesus, there is no evidence of salvation. After conversion, our God is our joy, comfort, guide, teacher, and in every sense our light. He is light within, light around, light reflected from us, and light to be revealed to us. He, then, who by faith has laid hold upon God, has all covenant blessings in his possession.

September 10

*S*urely if there is a happy verse in the Bible it is this: "My beloved is mine, and I am his" (Song 2:16). So peaceful, so full of assurance, so overrunning with happiness and contentment, is it that it might well have been written by the same hand which penned the Twenty-third Psalm. The verse savors of Him who, an hour before He went to Gethsemane, said, "Peace I leave with you, my peace I give unto you: not as the world giveth, give I unto you" (John 14:27), and, "In the world ye shall have tribulation: but be of good cheer; I have overcome the world" (John 16:33). Let us ring the silver bell again, for its notes are exquisitely sweet: "My beloved is mine, and I am his."

September 11

*N*o Christian is safe when his soul is slothful and his God is far from him. Every Christian is always safe as to the great matter of his standing in Christ, but he is not safe as regards his experience in holiness and communion with Jesus in this life. Satan does not often attack a Christian who is living near God. It is when the Christian departs from his God, becomes spiritually starved, and endeavors to feed on vanities, that the devil discovers his vantage hour. He may sometimes stand toe to toe with the child of God who is active in his Master's service, but the battle is generally short. Oh, for grace to walk humbly with our God!

September 12

*H*e draws us into closer communion with Himself. We have been sitting on the doorstep of God's house, and He bids us to advance into the banqueting hall and sup with Him. But, we decline the honor. There are secret rooms not yet opened to us; Jesus invites us to enter them, but we hold back. Shame on our cold hearts! We are but poor lovers of our sweet Lord Jesus, not fit to be His servants, much less to be His brides, and yet He has exalted us to be bone of His bone and flesh of His flesh, married to Him by a glorious marriage covenant. Herein is love!

September 13

*H*ow blessed to feel assured that the Lord is with us in all our ways and condescends to go down into our humiliations and banishments with us! Even beyond the ocean, our Father's love beams like the sun in its strength. We cannot hesitate to go where Jehovah promises His presence. "Fear not" is the Lord's command and His divine encouragement to those who at His bidding are launching upon new seas; the divine presence and preservation forbid so much as one unbelieving fear. Without our God, we should fear to move, but when He bids us go, it would be dangerous to tarry. Reader, go forward, and fear not.

September 14

*T*he love which the early Christians felt towards the Lord was not a quiet emotion which they hid within themselves in the secret chamber of their souls and which they only spoke of when they met on the first day of the week and sang hymns in honor of Christ Jesus the Crucified. It was, however, a passion within them of such a vehement and all-consuming energy that it was visible in their actions, spoken in their common talk, and seen in their eyes, even in their commonest glances. Love for Jesus was a flame which fed upon the core and heart of a believer's being, and, therefore, from its own force burned its way into the outer man and shone there.

September 15

Look at your possessions, believer, and compare your portion with the lot of your fellowmen. Some of them have their portion in the field. They are rich and their harvests yield them a golden increase, but what are harvests compared with your God who is the God of harvests? What are bursting granaries compared with Him, who is the Farmer and who feeds you with the bread of heaven? Some have their portion in the city. Their wealth is abundant and flows to them in constant streams until they become a very reservoir of gold, but what is gold compared with your God? "Thou art my portion, O LORD" (Ps. 119:57).

September 16

Jesus is the great teacher of lowliness of heart. We need daily to learn of Him. See the Master taking a towel and washing His disciples' feet! Follower of Christ, will you not humble yourself? See Him as the Servant of Servants, and surely you cannot be proud! "He humbled himself" (Phil. 2:8). Was He not on earth always stripping off first one robe of honor and then another until, naked, He was fastened to the cross? And there, did He not empty out His inmost self, pouring out His lifeblood, giving up all for us? How low was our dear Redeemer brought! How then can we be proud?

September 17

We would see Jesus.—John 12:21

*I*s this your condition, my reader, at this moment? Have you but one desire, and is that after Christ? Then you are not far from the kingdom of heaven. Have you but one wish in your heart, and is that one wish that you may be washed from all your sins in Jesus' blood? Can you really say, "I would give all I have to be a Christian; I would give up everything I have and hope for if I might but feel that I have an interest in Christ?" Then, despite all your fears, be of good cheer; the Lord loves you, and you will come out into daylight soon and rejoice in the liberty "wherewith Christ hath made us free" (Gal. 5:1).

September 18

*J*esus gave His blood for us; what will we give to Him? We are His, and all that we have, for He has purchased us into Himself—can we act as if we were our own? Oh, for more consecration! And to this end, oh, for more love! Blessed Jesus, You do receive with favor the smallest sincere token of affection! You do receive our poor forget-me-nots and love tokens as though they were intrinsically precious, though indeed they are but as the bunch of wild flowers which the child brings to its mother. We will give You the firstfruits of our increase and pay You tithes of all, and then we will confess "of thine own have we given thee" (1 Chron. 29:14).

September 19

*W*e have each of us peculiar gifts and special manifestations, but the one object God has in view is the perfecting of the whole body of Christ. We must, therefore, bring our spiritual possessions and lay them at the apostles' feet and distribute all of what God has given to us. Keep back no part of the precious truth, but speak what you know and testify what you have seen. Let not the toil, darkness, or possible unbelief of your friends weigh one moment in the scale. Get up and march to the place of duty; there tell what great things God has shown to your soul. We too must bear our witness concerning Jesus.

September 20

*I*t is well with the righteous—well upon divine authority. The mouth of God speaks the comforting assurance. Blessed be God for a faith which enables us to believe God when the creatures contradict Him. It is, says the Word, at all times well with you, righteous one (see Isaiah 3:10); then, beloved, if you cannot see it, let God's Word stand instead of sight. Yes, believe it on divine authority more confidently than if your eyes and your feeling told it to you. Whom God blesses is blessed indeed, and what His lip declares is truth most sure and steadfast.

September 21

*J*esus wears all the glory which the pomp of heaven can bestow upon Him, which ten thousand times ten thousand angels can minister to Him. You cannot with your utmost stretch of imagination conceive His exceeding greatness, yet there will be a further revelation of it when He will descend from heaven in great power with all the holy angels: "Then shall he sit upon the throne of his glory" (Matt. 25:31). Oh, the splendor of that glory! Nor is this the close, for eternity will sound His praise. "Thy throne, O God, is for ever and ever" (Ps. 45:6). Reader, if you would joy in Christ's glory hereafter, He must be glorious in your sight now. Is He so?

September 22

*W*hen the two disciples had reached Emmaus and were refreshing themselves at the evening meal, the mysterious stranger who had so enchanted them upon the road took bread and broke it, made Himself known to them, and then vanished out of their sight. They had constrained Him to abide with them, because the day was far spent, but now, although it was much later, their love was a lamp to their feet, yes, wings also. They forgot the darkness; their weariness was all gone. Forthwith, they journeyed back the threescore furlongs to tell the glad news of a risen Lord who had appeared to them by the way.

*G*od neither chose us nor called us because we were holy. He called us that we might be holy, and holiness is the beauty produced by His workmanship in us. The excellencies which we see in a believer are as much the work of God as the atonement itself. Thus is brought out very sweetly the fullness of the grace of God. Salvation must be of grace because the Lord is the author of it. Salvation must be of grace because the Lord works in such a manner that our righteousness is forever excluded. Such is the believer's privilege—a present salvation. Such is the evidence that he is called to it—a holy life.

*B*eliever do you remember that rapturous day when you first realized pardon through Jesus the Sin-bearer? Can you not make glad confession and say, "My soul recalls her day of deliverance with delight. Laden with guilt and full of fears, I saw my Savior as my Substitute, and I laid my hand upon Him; oh, how timidly at first, but courage grew, and confidence was confirmed until I leaned my soul entirely upon Him. Now it is my unceasing joy to know that my sins are no longer imputed to me but laid upon Him. Like the debts of the wounded traveler, Jesus, like the good Samaritan, has said of all my future sinfulness, 'Set that to My account.'"

*D*o you think, Christian, that you can measure the love of Christ? Think of what His love has brought you—justification, adoption, sanctification, eternal life! The riches of His goodness are unsearchable! Oh, the breadth of the love of Christ! Will such a love as this have half our hearts? Will Jesus' marvelous loving-kindness and tender care meet with but faint response and tardy acknowledgment? Oh my soul, tune your heart to a glad song of thanksgiving! Go through the day rejoicing, for you are no desolate wanderer but a beloved child, watched over, cared for, supplied, and defended by your Lord.

*E*ndeavor to know the Father. Bury your head in His bosom in deep repentance, and confess that you are not worthy to be called His son. Receive the kiss of His love; let the ring which is the token of His eternal faithfulness be on your finger. Sit at His table, and let your heart make merry in His grace. Then, press forward, and seek to know much of the Son of God. Know Him as eternal God and yet suffering, finite man; follow Him as He walks the waters with the tread of deity and as He sits upon the well in the weariness of humanity. Be not satisfied unless you know much of Jesus Christ as your Friend, your Brother, your Husband, your all.

September 27

*H*e is full of truth. True have His promises been; not one has failed. I want none beside Him. In life He is my life, and in death He will be the death of death. In poverty Christ is my riches; in sickness He makes my bed; in darkness He is my star; and in brightness He is my sun. He is the manna of the camp in the wilderness, and He will be the new corn of the host when they come to Canaan. Jesus is to me all grace and no wrath, all truth and no falsehood, and of truth and grace He is full, infinitely full. My soul, this day, bless with all your might the Only Begotten.

September 28

*H*ow comprehensive is the love of Jesus! There is no part of His people's interests which He does not consider, and there is nothing which concerns their welfare which is not important to Him. "The steps of a good man are ordered by the LORD: and he delighteth in his way" (Ps. 37:23). Believer, rest assured that the heart of Jesus cares about your meaner affairs. The breadth of His tender love is such that you may resort to Him in all matters, for in all your afflictions He is afflicted. "Like as a father pitieth his children" (Ps. 103:13), so does He pity you. The meanest interests of all His saints are all borne upon the broad bosom of the Son of God.

September 29

Our God's tender love for His servants makes Him concerned for the state of their inward feelings. He desires them to be of good courage. Some esteem it a small thing for a believer to be vexed with doubts and fears, but God thinks not so. Our Master does not think so lightly of our unbelief as we do. Our Lord does not love to see our countenance sad. It was a law of Ahasuerus that no one should come into the king's court dressed in mourning. This is not the law of the King of Kings, for we may come mourning as we are, but still He would have us put off "the spirit of heaviness" and put on "the garment of praise," (Isa. 61:3) for there is much reason to rejoice.

September 30

If his dark nights are as bright as the world's days, what will his days be? If even his starlight is more splendid than the sun, what must his sunlight be? If he can praise the Lord in the fires, how will he extol Him before the eternal throne! If evil is good to him now, what will the overflowing goodness of God be to him then? Oh, blessed "afterward"! Who would not be a Christian? Who would not bear the present cross for the crown which comes afterwards? But herein is work for patience, for the rest is not for today, nor the triumph for the present, but "afterward." Wait, soul, and "let patience have her perfect work" (James 1:4).

October 1

*W*hat is your desire this day? Is it set upon heavenly things? Do you desire liberty in close communication with God? Do you aspire to know the heights and depths and lengths and breadths? Then you must draw near to Jesus; you must get a clear sight of Him in His preciousness and completeness. He who understands Christ receives an anointing from the Holy One by which he knows all things. Are you saying, "Oh, that He would dwell in my bosom! Would that He would make my heart His dwelling-place forever"? Open the door, beloved, and He will come into your souls. He has long been knocking, and He will sup with you, and you with him. (See Revelation 3:20.)

October 2

*P*oor souls! Forget not the present Savior who bids you to look to Him and be saved. He could heal you at once, but you prefer to wait for an angel and a wonder. To trust Him is a sure way to every blessing, and He is worthy of the most implicit confidence. But, unbelief makes you prefer the cold porches of Bethesda to the warm bosom of His love. Oh, that the Lord may turn His eye upon the multitudes who are in this state today. May He forgive the slights which they have put upon His divine power and call them by that sweet, constraining voice to rise from their beds of despair and, in the energy of faith, take up their beds and walk. (See John 5:8.)

October 3

Christians are not to be praised for neglected duties under the pretense of having secret fellowship with Jesus. It is not sitting, but sitting at Jesus' feet, which is commendable. Do not think that activity is in itself an evil; it is a great blessing and a means of grace to us. Those who have most fellowship with Christ are not recluses or hermits but indefatigable laborers who are toiling for Jesus and who, in their toil, have Him side by side with them so that they are workers together with God. Let us remember, then, in anything we have to do for Jesus that we can do it, and should do it, in close communion with Him.

October 4

We must manifest the spirit of Christ in meekness, gentleness, and forgiveness. Let us search and see if we truly suffer with Jesus. And if we do thus suffer, what is our "light affliction" (2 Cor. 4:17) compared with reigning with Him? Oh, it is so blessed to be in the furnace with Christ and such an honor to stand in the pillory with Him that if there were no future reward, we might count ourselves happy in present honor. But, when the recompense is so eternal, so infinitely more than we had any right to expect, should we not take up the cross with alacrity and go on our way rejoicing?

October 5

*H*e has been good to me in all my needs, trials, struggles, and sorrows. Never could there be a better Master, for His service is freedom, His rule is love. The ancient saints proved Him to be a good Master, and each of them rejoiced to sing, "I am Your servant, Lord!" I will bear this witness before my friends and neighbors, for possibly they may be led by my testimony to seek my Lord Jesus as their Master. Oh, that they would do so! They would never repent so wise a deed. If they would but take His easy yoke, they would find themselves in so royal a service that they would enlist in it forever.

October 6

*M*y soul, hearken to the voice of your God. He is always ready to speak with you when you are prepared to hear. If there is any slowness to commune, it is not on His part but altogether on your own, for He stands at the door and knocks, and if His people will but open, He rejoices to enter. (See Revelation 3:20.) But in what state is my heart, which is my Lord's garden? May I venture to hope that it is bringing forth fruit fit for Him? If not, He will have much to reprove, but still I pray for Him to come to me, for nothing can so certainly bring my heart into a right condition as the presence of the Sun of Righteousness who brings healing in His wings. (See Malachi 4:2.)

October 7

*H*e sups with you because you open the house or the heart, and you with Him because He brings the provision. He could not sup with you if it were not in your heart, nor could you sup with Him if He did not bring the provision with Him. Fling wide, then, the portals of your soul. He will come with that love which you long to feel; He will come with that joy into which you cannot work your poor depressed spirit; He will bring the peace which now you do not have. Only open the door to Him, and He will dwell there forever. Oh, wondrous love, that brings such a Guest to dwell in such a heart!

October 8

*F*aith in Jesus is more than a match for worldly trials, temptations, and unbelief, and it overcomes them all. The same absorbing principle shines in the faithful service of God. With an enthusiastic love for Jesus, difficulties are surmounted, sacrifices become pleasures, sufferings are honors. But if religion is thus a consuming passion in the heart, then it follows that there are many people who profess religion but have it not, for what they have will not bear this test. Examine yourself, my reader, on this point. Aaron's rod proved its heaven-given power. Is your religion doing so? If Christ be anything, He must be everything. Oh, rest not until love and faith in Jesus are the master passions of your soul!

October 9

*I*t is well with the righteous always. From the beginning of the year to the end of the year, from the first gathering of evening shadows until the day-star shines, in all conditions, and under all circumstances, it will be well with the righteous. It is so well with him that we could not imagine it to be better. He is well fed; he feeds upon the flesh and blood of Jesus. He is well clothed; he wears the imputed righteousness of Christ. He is well housed; he dwells in God. He is well married; his soul is knit in bonds of marriage union to Christ. He is well provided for, for the Lord is his Shepherd. He is well endowed, for heaven is his inheritance.

October 10

*S*hould it happen that, in the providence of God, you are a loser by conscience, you will find that if the Lord does not pay you back in the silver of earthly prosperity, He will discharge His promise in the gold of spiritual joy. Remember that a man's life consists not in the abundance of that which he possesses. To wear a guileless spirit, to have a heart void of offense, and to have the favor and smile of God, are greater riches than the mines of Ophir could yield or the traffic of Tyre could win. "Better is a dinner of herbs where love is, than a stalled ox and hatred therewith" (Prov. 15:17). An ounce of heart's-ease is worth a ton of gold.

October 11

*W*e must not imagine that we are suffering for Christ, and with Christ, if we are not in Christ. Beloved friend, are you trusting to Jesus only? If not, whatever you may have to mourn over on earth, you are not suffering with Christ and have no hope of reigning with Him in heaven. Neither are we to conclude that all a Christian's sufferings are sufferings with Christ, for it is essential that he is called by God to suffer. If we are rash and imprudent, and run into positions for which neither providence nor grace has fitted us, we ought to question whether we are not sinning rather than communing with Jesus.

October 12

*C*ome, Lord, my God. My soul invites you earnestly and waits for you eagerly. Come to me, Jesus, my Well Beloved, and plant fresh flowers in my garden such as I see blooming in such perfection in Your matchless character! Come, my Father, who is the Husbandman, and deal with me in your tenderness and prudence! Come, Holy Spirit, and bedew my whole nature, as the herbs are now moistened with the evening dews. Oh, that God would speak to me! "Speak, LORD; for thy servant heareth" (1 Sam. 3:9). Oh, that He would walk with me; I am ready to give up my whole heart and mind to Him. I am only asking what He delights to give.

October 13

*G*od is glorified by our serving Him in our proper vocations. Every lawful trade may be sanctified by Scripture to noblest ends. Turn to the Bible, and you will find the most menial forms of labor connected either with the most daring deeds of faith or with people whose lives have been illustrious for holiness. Therefore, do not be discontented with your calling. Whatever God has made your position, or your work, abide in that unless you are quite sure that He calls you to something else. Let your first care be to glorify God to the utmost of your power where you are. Fill your present sphere to His praise, and if He needs you in another, He will show it to you.

October 14

*N*o human mind can adequately estimate the infinite value of the divine sacrifice, for great as is the sin of God's people, the atonement which takes it away is immeasurably greater. Therefore, the believer, even when sin rolls like a black flood and the remembrance of the past is bitter, can yet stand before the blazing throne of the great and holy God and cry, "Who is he that condemneth? It is Christ that died, yea rather, that is risen again" (Rom. 8:34). While the recollection of his sin fills him with shame and sorrow, he at the same time makes it a foil to show the brightness of mercy. Guilt is the dark night in which the fair star of divine love shines with serene splendor.

October 15

*I*t is a happy thing when we can address the Lord with the confidence which David manifests. It gives us great power in prayer and comfort in trial. "On thee do I wait all the day" (Ps. 25:5). Patience is the fair handmaid and daughter of faith; we cheerfully wait when we are certain that we will not wait in vain. It is our duty and our privilege to wait upon the Lord in service, in worship, in expectancy, and in trust all the days of our life. Our faith will be tried faith, and if it be of the true kind, it will bear continued trial without yielding. We will not grow weary of waiting upon God if we remember how long and how graciously He once waited for us.

October 16

*S*eeing that we have such a God to trust, let us rest upon Him with all our weight. Let us resolutely drive out all unbelief and endeavor to get rid of doubts and fears which so much mar our comfort since there is no excuse for fear where God is the foundation of our trust. A loving parent would be sorely grieved if his child could not trust him, and how ungenerous, how unkind, is our conduct when we put so little confidence in our heavenly Father who has never failed us and who never will! We have been in many trials, but we have never yet been cast where we could not find in our God all that we needed.

October 17

He appeared first to Mary Magdalene.—Mark 16:9

*I*f we would see much of Christ, let us serve Him. Tell me who they are that sit most often under the banner of His love and drink deepest draughts from the cup of communion, and I am sure they will be those who give most, who serve best, and who abide closest to the bleeding heart of their dear Lord. But notice how Christ revealed Himself to this sorrowing one—by a word, "Mary." She needed but one word in His voice, and at once she knew Him. Her heart admitted allegiance by another word. Her heart was too full to say more. That one word most fitting implies obedience. She said, "Master." (See John 20:16.)

October 18

*C*hristian man! Learn to comfort yourself in God's gracious dealing toward the church. That which is so dear to your Master, should it not be dear above all else to you? What, though your way is dark, can you not gladden your heart with the triumphs of His Cross and the spread of His truth? Our own personal troubles are forgotten while we look, not only upon what God *has* done and *is* doing for Zion but on the glorious things He *will yet do* for His church. Try the following, believer, whenever you are sad of heart and in heaviness of spirit: "Pray for the peace of Jerusalem" (Ps. 122:6), and your own soul will be refreshed.

October 19

*G*od is for me" (Ps. 56:9). He was "for us," or He would not have given His well-beloved Son. And because He is "for us," the voice of prayer will always ensure His help. "When I cry unto thee, then shall mine enemies turn back" (Ps. 56:9). This is no uncertain hope but a well-grounded assurance— "this I know" (Ps. 56:9). I will direct my prayer to You and will look up for the answer, assured that it will come, for "God is for me." Oh, believer, how happy are you with the King of Kings on your side. How safe with such a protector! How sure your cause, pleaded by such an advocate! If God is for you, who can be against you? (See Romans 8:31.)

October 20

*T*he blood of Jesus Christ his Son cleanseth us from all sin" (1 John 1:7), not only from sin but "from all sin." Reader, I cannot tell you the exceeding sweetness of this word, but I pray that God the Holy Spirit will give you a taste of it. Manifold are our sins against God. Whether the bill is little or great, the same receipt can discharge one as well as the other. The blood of Jesus Christ is as blessed and divine a payment for the transgressions of blaspheming Peter as for the shortcomings of loving John. Our iniquity is gone, all gone at once, and all gone forever. Blessed completeness! What a sweet theme to dwell upon as one begins another day.

October 21

*A*s a true believer, called by grace and washed in the precious blood of Jesus, you have tasted of better drink than the river of this world's pleasure can give you. You have had fellowship with Christ; you have obtained the joy of seeing Jesus and leaning your head upon His bosom. Do the trifles, the songs, the honors, the merriment of this earth content you after that? If you are wandering after the waters of Egypt, oh, return quickly to the one living fountain. The waters of Sihor may be sweet to the Egyptians, but they will prove only bitterness to you. What do you have to do with them? Jesus asks you this question—what will you answer Him?

October 22

Why go I mourning?—Psalm 42:9

*C*an you answer this, believer? Can't you find any reason why you are so often mourning instead of rejoicing? Why yield to gloomy anticipations? Who told you that the night would never end in day? Who told you that the winter of your discontent would proceed from frost to frost, from snow, ice, and hail to deeper snow and yet more heavy tempest of despair? Know you not that day follows night, that flood comes after ebb, that spring and summer succeed to winter? Have hope! For God fails you not.

*I*f there is one place where our Lord Jesus most fully becomes the joy and comfort of His people, it is where He plunged deepest into the depths of woe. Come hither, gracious souls, and behold the Man in the garden of Gethsemane. Behold His heart so brimming with love that He cannot hold it in—so full of sorrow that it must find a vent. Behold the Man as they drive the nails into His hands and feet. Look up, repenting sinners, and see the sorrowful image of your suffering Lord. If we would live aright, it must be by the contemplation of His death; if we would rise to dignity, it must be by considering His humiliation and His sorrow.

*W*ho shall lay any thing to the charge of God's elect?" (Rom. 8:33). Most blessed challenge! How unanswerable it is! Every sin of the elect was laid upon the great Champion of our salvation and, by the atonement, carried away. There is no sin in God's book against His people. When the guilt of sin was taken away, the punishment of sin was removed. For the Christian, there is no stroke from God's angry hand—no, not so much as a single frown of justice. The believer may be chastised by his Father, but God the Judge has nothing to say to the Christian except, "I have absolved you; you are acquitted."

October 25

And the evening and the morning were the first day.
—Genesis 1:5

*T*he evening was "darkness" and the morning was "light," and yet the two together are called by the name that is given to the light alone! In every believer there is darkness and light; however, he is not a sinner because there is sin in him, but he is a saint because he possesses some degree of holiness. This will be a most comforting thought to those who ask, "Can I be a child of God while there is so much darkness in me?" Yes, for you, like the day, take not your name from the evening but from the morning, and you are spoken of in the Word of God as if you were even now perfectly holy.

October 26

*O*f the Savior, and only of the Savior, is it true in the fullest, broadest, and most unqualified sense: He "went about doing good" (Acts 10:38). From this description it is evident that He did good personally. The evangelists constantly tell us that He touched the leper with His own finger, that He anointed the eyes of the blind, and that, in cases where He was asked to speak the word only at a distance, He did not usually comply but went Himself to the sick bed and there personally wrought the cure. A lesson to us, if He would do good, we should do it ourselves. He has left us an example that we should follow in His steps.

October 27

I give unto [my sheep]," says He, "eternal life; and they shall never perish, neither shall any man pluck them out of my hand" (John 10:28). What do you say to this, trembling, feeble mind? Is not this a precious mercy, that in coming to Christ you do not come to one who will treat you well for a little while and then send you away. He will receive you and make you His bride, and you will be His forever. Receive no longer the spirit of bondage again to fear but the spirit of adoption whereby you will cry, Abba, Father! (See Romans 8:15.) Oh, the grace of these words, "I will in no wise cast out" (John 6:37).

October 28

Thou crownest the year with thy goodness.—Psalm 65:11

*A*ll the year round, every hour of every day, God is richly blessing us; both when we sleep and when we wake, His mercy waits upon us. The sun may leave us a legacy of darkness, but our God never ceases to shine upon His children with beams of love. Like a river, His loving-kindness is always flowing with a fullness as inexhaustible as His own nature. Like the atmosphere which constantly surrounds the earth and is always ready to support the life of man, the benevolence of God surrounds all His creatures. In it, as in their element, they "live, and move, and have [their] being" (Acts 17:28).

*I*f the most precious are tried in the fire, are we to escape the crucible? If the diamond must be vexed upon the wheel, are we to be made perfect without suffering? Who has commanded the wind to cease from blowing because our ship is on the deep? Why, and wherefore, should we be treated better than our Lord? The Firstborn felt the rod, and why not the younger brothers? It is pride which would choose a downy pillow and a silken couch for a soldier of the cross. Wiser far is he who, being first resigned to the divine will, grows by the energy of grace to be pleased with it and so learns to gather lilies at the foot of the cross and, like Samson, to find honey in the lion.

October 30

*I*f our Lord is so ready to heal the sick and bless the needy, then, my soul, be not slow to put yourself in His way that He may smile on you. Do not be slack in asking, if He is so abundant in bestowing. Give earnest heed to His Word now, that Jesus may speak through it to your heart. Where He is to be found, there make your resort that you may obtain His blessing. When He is present to heal, may He not heal you? But surely He is present even now, for He always comes to hearts which need Him. And do you not need? Ah, He knows how much!

Son of David, turn Your eyes and look upon the distress which is now before You, and make Your supplicant whole.

The LORD trieth the righteous.—Psalm 11:5

*A*ll events are under the control of Providence; consequently all the trials of our outward life are traceable at once to the great First Cause. All providential occurrences are doors to trials. Even our mercies, like roses, have their thorns. Our mountains are not too high and our valleys are not too low for temptations. Trials lurk on all roads. Everywhere, above and beneath, we are beset and surrounded with dangers. Yet no shower falls unpermitted from the threatening cloud; every drop has its order before it hastens to the earth. The trials which come from God are sent to prove and strengthen us.

November 1

*L*et me commend to you a life of trust in God in temporal things. Walk in your path of integrity with steadfast steps, and show that you are invincibly strong in the strength which confidence in God alone can confer. Thus, you will be delivered from burdensome care; you will not be troubled with evil tidings. Your heart will be fixed, trusting in the Lord. How pleasant to float along the stream of providence! There is no more blessed way of living than a life of dependence upon a covenant-keeping God. We have no care, for He cares for us; we have no troubles because we cast our burdens upon the Lord.

November 2

*H*eal my soul; for I have sinned against thee" (Ps. 41:4). For this also the godly praise the name of the Lord, saying, "He heals all our diseases." (See Psalm 103:1–3.) What a transcendent comfort it is that in the person of Jesus "dwelleth all the fulness of the Godhead bodily" (Col. 2:9). My soul, whatever your disease may be, this great Physician can heal you. If He is God, there can be no limit to His power. Come just as you are, for He who is God can certainly restore you from your plague. None will restrain the healing virtue which proceeds from Jesus our Lord. All His patients have been cured in the past and will be in the future, and you will be one among them, my friend, if you will but rest yourself in Him.

November 3

If we walk in the light, as he is in the light....
—1 John 1:7

*A*s He is in the light! Can we ever attain to this? Will we ever be able to walk as clearly in the light as He whom we call "Our Father" is, of whom it is written, "God is light, and in him is no darkness at all" (1 John 1:5)? Certainly, this is the model which is set before us, for the Savior Himself said, "Be ye therefore perfect, even as your Father which is in heaven is perfect" (Matt. 5:48). Although we may feel that we can never rival the perfection of God, we are yet to seek after it and never be satisfied until we attain to it.

November 4

*F*or thou art my strength" (Ps. 31:4). What an inexpressible sweetness is to be found in these few words! How joyfully may we encounter toils, and how cheerfully may we endure sufferings, when we can lay hold upon celestial strength. He is a happy man who has such matchless might engaged upon his side. Our own strength would be of little service when embarrassed in the nets of base cunning, but the Lord's strength is ever available. We have but to invoke it, and we will find it near at hand. If by faith we are depending alone upon the strength of the mighty God of Israel, we may use our holy reliance as a plea in supplication.

*T*hough we have brought forth some fruit for Christ and have a joyful hope that we are plants of His own right-hand planting, yet there are times when we feel very barren. Prayer is lifeless; love is cold; faith is weak. Each grace in the garden of our heart languishes and droops. We are like flowers in the hot sun requiring the refreshing shower. In such a condition what are we to do? "Sing, O barren...break forth into singing, and cry aloud" (Isa. 54:1). Sing, believer, for it will cheer your own heart and the hearts of other desolate ones. Sing on, for now that God makes you loath to be without fruit, He will soon cover you with clusters.

November 6

Ourselves also, which have the firstfruits of the Spirit.
—Romans 8:23

*B*ut the firstfruits were not the harvest, and the works of the Spirit in us at this moment are not the consummation—the perfection is yet to come. We must not boast that we have attained and so reckon the wheat for the wave offering to be all the produce of the year; we must hunger and thirst after righteousness and pant for the day of full redemption. Dear reader, this day open your heart wide, and God will fill it. Groan within yourself for higher degrees of consecration, and your Lord will grant them to you, for He is able "to do exceeding abundantly above all that we ask or think" (Eph. 3:20).

November 7

*G*od makes no difference in His love to His children. A child is a child to Him. He will not make him a hired servant, but he will feast upon the fatted calf and will have the music and the dancing as much as if he had never gone astray. No chains are worn in the court of King Jesus. Our admission into full privileges may be gradual, but it is sure. Perhaps our reader is saying, "I wish I could enjoy the promises and walk at liberty in my Lord's commands." "If thou believest with all thine heart, thou mayest" (Acts 8:37). Loose the chains of your neck, captive daughter (Isa. 52:2), for Jesus makes you free.

November 8

*T*o know Christ and be found in Him—oh, this is life, this is joy, this is marrow and fatness. His unsearchable riches will be best known in eternity. He will give you, on the way to heaven, all you need. Your place of defense will be the ramparts of rocks. Your bread will be given to you, and your waters will be sure. But, it is there, there, where you will hear the song of them that triumph, the shout of them that feast, and will see the glorious and beloved One. The unsearchable riches of Christ! Lord, teach us more and more of Jesus, and we will tell out the good news to others.

November 9

*B*eyond measure it is desirable that we, as believers, should have the person of Jesus constantly before us to inflame our love towards Him and to increase our knowledge of Him. But to have Jesus ever near, the heart must be full of Him, welling up with His love, even to overflowing; hence, the apostle prays "that Christ may dwell in your hearts" (Eph. 3:17). See how near he would have Jesus to be! "That He may dwell," not that He may call upon you sometimes, as a casual visitor enters into a house and tarries for a night, but that He may "dwell," that Jesus may become the Lord and Tenant of your heart.

November 10

*T*he believer commits his soul to the hand of his God. It came from Him; it is His own. He has before time sustained it. He is able to keep it, and it is most fit that He should receive it. All things are safe in Jehovah's hands. What we entrust to the Lord will be secure, both now and in that day of days towards which we are hastening. It is peaceful living and glorious dying to repose in the care of heaven. At all times we should commit our all to Jesus' faithful hand; then, though life may hang on a thread and adversities may multiply as the sands of the sea, our soul will dwell at ease and delight itself in quiet resting places.

November 11

The bow shall be seen in the cloud.—Genesis 9:14

*W*hen may we expect to see the token of the covenant? The rainbow is only to be seen painted upon a cloud. Beloved, our God, who is as the sun to us, always shines, but we do not always see Him. Clouds hide His face, but no matter what drops may be falling, or what clouds may be threatening, if He does but shine there will be a rainbow at once. It is said that when we see the rainbow, the shower is over. Certain it is that when Christ comes our troubles remove; when we behold Jesus, our sins vanish and our debts and fears subside. When Jesus walks the waters of the sea, how profound the calm!

November 12

*T*he bow shall be in the cloud; and I will look upon it, that I may remember the everlasting covenant" (Gen. 9:16). Oh, it is not *my* remembering God, it is God's remembering *me* which is the ground of my safety. It is not *my* laying hold of His covenant, but His covenant's laying hold on *me*. Glory be to God! The whole of the bulwarks of salvation are secured by divine power, and even the minor towers, which we may imagine might have been left to man, are guarded by almighty strength. Even the remembrance of the covenant is not left to our memories, for we might forget, but our Lord cannot forget the saints whom He has engraved on the palms of His hands. (See Isaiah 49:16.)

*B*ehold one of the great Physician's mightiest arts; He has power to forgive sin! Before the ransom had been paid, before the blood had been literally sprinkled on the mercy seat, He had power to forgive sin. Does He not have power to do it now that He has died? He has boundless power now that He has finished transgression and made an end of sin. Hear Him pleading before the eternal Father, pointing to His wounds, urging the merit of His sacred passion! What power to forgive is here! He is exalted on high to give repentance and remission of sins. The most crimson sins are removed by the crimson of His blood.

November 14

And I will give you an heart of flesh.—Ezekiel 36:26

*T*he hard heart does not love the Redeemer, but the renewed heart burns with affection towards Him. Many are the privileges of this renewed heart: it is here the Spirit dwells, it is here that Jesus rests. It is fitted to receive every spiritual blessing, and every blessing comes to it. It is prepared to yield every heavenly fruit to the honor and praise of God, and, therefore, the Lord delights in it. A tender heart is the best defense against sin and the best preparation for heaven. A renewed heart stands on its water tower looking for the coming of the Lord Jesus. Have you this heart of flesh?

November 15

*T*here is no elevation of grace, no attainment of spirituality, no clearness of assurance, no post of duty, which is not open to you if you have but the power to believe. Lay aside your sackcloth and ashes and rise to the dignity of your true position. The golden throne of assurance is waiting for you! The crown of communion with Jesus is ready to bedeck your brow. Wrap yourself in scarlet and fine linen and fare sumptuously every day. If you believe, your land will flow with milk and honey, and your soul will be satisfied as with marrow and fatness. (See Exodus 3:8; Psalm 63:5.) Gather golden sheaves of grace, for they await you in the fields of faith. "All things are possible to him that believeth" (Mark 9:23).

November 16

I said not unto the seed of Jacob, Seek ye me in vain.
—Isaiah 45:19

*G*od has clearly revealed that He will hear the prayer of those who call upon Him, and that declaration cannot be contravened. He was so firmly, so truthfully, so righteously spoken, that there can be no room for doubt. He does not reveal His mind in unintelligible words, but He speaks plainly and positively, "Ask, and ye shall receive" (John 16:24). Believe, trembler, this sure truth: that prayer must and will be heard and that never, even in the secrets of eternity, has the Lord said to any living soul, "Seek Me in vain."

*S*ince the first hour in which goodness came into conflict with evil, it has never ceased to be true in spiritual experience that Satan hinders us. If we toil in the field, he seeks to break the plowshare. If we build the wall, he labors to cast down the stones. If we would serve God in suffering or in conflict, everywhere Satan hinders us. He hinders us when we are first coming to Jesus Christ. Fierce conflicts we had with Satan when we first looked to the cross and lived. Now that we are saved, he endeavors to hinder the completeness of our personal character. "Let him that thinketh he standeth take heed lest he fall" (1 Cor. 10:12).

November 18

*A*t this moment, dear reader, whatever your sinfulness, Christ has power to pardon—power to pardon you and millions such as you are. A word will accomplish it. He has nothing more to do to win your pardon; all the atoning work is done. He can, in answer to your tears, forgive your sins today and make you know it. He can breathe into your soul at this very moment a peace with God "which passeth all understanding" (Phil. 4:7), which will spring from perfect remission of your manifold iniquities. Do you believe that? I trust that you believe it. May you experience now the power of Jesus to forgive sin!

*B*ounteous is Jehovah in His nature; to give is His delight. His gifts are precious beyond measure and are as freely given as the light of the sun. He gives grace to His elect because He wills it, to His redeemed because of His covenant, to the called because of His promise, to believers because they seek it, and to sinners because they need it. He gives grace abundantly, seasonably, constantly, readily, and sovereignly, doubly enhancing the value of the boon by the manner of its bestowal. Reader, how blessed it is, as the years roll round and the leaves begin again to fall, to enjoy such an unfading promise as this: "The LORD will give grace" (Ps. 84:11).

November 20

*T*he dispensation of the old covenant was that of distance. When God appeared even to His servant Moses, He said, "Draw not nigh hither: put off thy shoes from off thy feet" (Exod. 3:5), and when He manifested himself upon Mount Sinai to His own chosen and separated people, one of the first commands was, "Thou shalt set bounds [about the mount]" (Exod. 19:12). When the Gospel came, we were placed on quite another footing. The word "go" was exchanged for "come." Distance was made to give place to nearness, and we who before time were far off were "made nigh by the blood of Christ" (Eph. 2:13). "Come unto me, all ye that labour and are heavy laden, and I will give you rest" (Matt. 11:28).

November 21

Oh, how precious is Christ! How can it be that I have thought so little of Him! How is it I can go abroad for joy and comfort when He is so full, so rich, so satisfying? Fellow believer, make a covenant with your heart, and ask your Lord to ratify it. Bid Him set you as a signet upon His finger and as a bracelet upon His arm. The sparrow has made a house, and the swallow a nest for herself where she may lay her young. So too would I make my nest, my home, in You. Never from You may the soul of Your turtle dove go forth again, but may I nestle close to You, Jesus, my true and only rest.

November 22

God employs His people to encourage one another. We should be glad that God usually works for man by man. It forms a bond of brotherhood, and being mutually dependent on one another, we are fused more completely into one family. Brothers, take the text as God's message to you. Aim to comfort the sorrowful and to animate the despondent. "Speak a word in season to him that is weary" (Isa. 50:4), and encourage those who are fearful to go on their way with gladness. God encourages you by His promises, Christ encourages you as He points to the heaven He has won for you, and the Spirit encourages you as He works in you to will and to do of His own will and pleasure (Phil. 2:13).

*M*ost of us know what it is to be overwhelmed in heart. Disappointments and heartbreaks will do this when billow after billow rolls over us, and we are like a broken shell hurled to and fro by the surf. Blessed be God at such seasons we are not without an all-sufficient solace. Our God is the harbor of weather-beaten sails, the hospice of forlorn pilgrims. Higher than we are is He. His mercy is higher than our sins, and His love is higher than our thoughts. He is a rock since He changes not, and He is a high rock because the tempests which overwhelm us roll far beneath at His feet. Oh, Lord, our God, by Your Holy Spirit, teach us Your way of faith, and lead us into Your rest.

November 24

*V*ery bitter is the enmity of the world against the people of Christ. Men will forgive a thousand faults in others, but they will magnify the most trivial offense in the follower of Jesus. Instead of vainly regretting this, let us turn it to account. Since so many are watching for our stumbling, let this be a special motive for walking very carefully before God. If we live carelessly, the lynx-eyed world will soon see it, and they will shout triumphantly, "See how these Christians act!" The Cross of Christ is in itself an offense to the world; let us take heed that we add no offense of our own, for thus can much damage be done to the cause of Christ and much insult offered to His name.

*D*oes Christ receive us when we come to Him, notwithstanding all our past sinfulness? Does He never chide us for having tried all other refuges first? And is there none on earth like Him? Is He the best of all the good, the fairest of all the fair? Oh, then let us praise Him! Daughters of Jerusalem, extol him with timbrel and harp! Now let the standards of pomp and pride be trampled under foot, but let the cross of Jesus, which the world frowns and scoffs at, be lifted on high. Oh, for a throne of ivory for our King! Let Him be set on high forever, and let my soul sit at His footstool and kiss His feet and wash them with my tears.

November 26

*T*his man receiveth sinners" (Luke 15:2) not, however, that they may remain sinners, but He receives them that He may pardon their sins, justify their persons, cleanse their hearts by His purifying Word, preserve their souls by the indwelling of the Holy Spirit, and enable them to serve Him, to show forth His praise, and to have communion with Him. Into His heart's love, He receives sinners, takes them from darkness, and wears them as jewels in His crown. He plucks them as brands from the burning and preserves them as costly monuments of His mercy. None are so precious in Jesus' sight as the sinners for whom He died.

November 27

*S*uccess is certain when the Lord has promised it. Although you may have pleaded month after month without evidence of answer, it is not possible that the Lord should be deaf when His people are earnest in a matter which concerns His glory. Delayed answers often set the heart searching itself and so lead to contrition and spiritual reformation. Reader, do not fall into the sin of unbelief, but continue in prayer and watching. Plead the precious blood with unceasing importunity, and it will be with you according to your desire.

November 28

*W*e are none of us so much awake as we should be. With a perishing world around us, to sleep is cruel. Oh, that we may leave forever the couch of ease and go forth with flaming torches to meet the coming Bridegroom! "My heart waketh" (Song 5:2). This is a happy sign. Life is not extinct, though sadly smothered. When our renewed hearts struggle against our natural heaviness, we should be grateful to sovereign grace for keeping a little vitality within the body of this death. Jesus will hear our hearts, will help our hearts, will visit our hearts, for the voice of the wakeful heart is really the voice of our Beloved saying, "Open to me" (Song 5:2). Holy zeal will surely unbar the door.

*I*n the evening of the day, opportunities are plentiful; men return from their labor, and the zealous soul-winner finds time to tell abroad the love of Jesus. Have I no evening work for Jesus? If I have not, let me no longer withhold my hand from a service which requires abundant labor. Jesus gave both His hands to the nails; how can I keep back one of mine from his blessed work? Night and day He toiled and prayed for me; how can I give a single hour to selfish indulgence? Up, idle heart; stretch out your hand to work, or uplift it to pray. Heaven and hell are in earnest; let me be so and this evening sow good seed for the Lord my God.

November 30

Now on whom dost thou trust?—Isaiah 36:5

*R*eader, this is an important question. Listen to the Christian's answer, and see if it is yours. "On whom dost thou trust?" "I trust," says the Christian, "*the Son*—the man, Christ Jesus. I trust in Him to take away all my sins by His own sacrifice and to adorn me with His perfect righteousness. I trust Him to be my Intercessor, to present my prayers and desires before His Father's throne, and I trust Him to be my Advocate at the last great day, to plead my cause, and to justify me. I trust Him for what He is, for what He has done, and for what He has promised yet to do."

December 1

*T*his age is peculiarly the dispensation of the Holy Spirit in which Jesus cheers us not by His personal presence, as He will do by and by, but by the indwelling and constant abiding of the Holy Spirit who is evermore the Comforter of the church. It is His office to console the hearts of God's people. He convinces of sin. He illuminates and instructs, but still the main part of His work lies in making glad the hearts of the renewed, in confirming the weak, and in lifting up all those who are bowed down. He does this by revealing Jesus to them. The Holy Spirit consoles, but Christ is the consolation.

December 2

*I*s, then, your calling a high calling? Has it ennobled your heart and set it upon heavenly things? Has it elevated your hopes, your tastes, your desires? If man alone calls you, you are uncalled. Is your calling of God? Is it a call to heaven as well as from heaven? Unless you are a stranger here, and heaven your home, you have not been called with a heavenly calling, for those who have been so called declare that they look "for a city which hath foundations, whose builder and maker is God" (Heb. 11:10). Is your calling thus holy, high, heavenly? Then, beloved, you have been called of God, for such is the calling wherewith God does call His people.

December 3

*M*any, in waiting upon the Lord, find immediate delight, but this is not the case with all. A deeper sense of sin may be given to you instead of a sense of pardon, and in such a case you will have need of patience to bear the heavy blow. Ah, poor heart, though Christ beat and bruise you, or even slay you, trust Him; though He should give you an angry word, believe in the love of His heart. Do not, I beseech you, give up seeking or trusting my Master because you have not yet obtained the conscious joy which you long for. Cast yourself on Him, and perseveringly depend, even where you cannot rejoicingly hope.

December 4

If any man sin, we have an advocate with the Father, Jesus Christ the righteous.—1 John 2:1

*W*hat words of tenderness, what sentences of persuasion, will the Anointed use when He stands up to plead for me! "Jesus Christ the righteous." This is not only His character but His plea. It is His character, and if the Righteous One is my advocate, then my cause is good or He would not have espoused it. It is His plea, for He meets the charge of unrighteousness against me by the plea that He is righteous. He declares Himself my substitute and puts His obedience to my account. My soul, you have a friend well fitted to be your advocate. He cannot but succeed. Leave yourself entirely in His hands.

December 5

*D*o not dissociate Jesus from our common manhood. It is a dark room which you are going through, but Jesus went through it before. It is a sharp fight which you are waging, but Jesus has stood toe to toe with the same enemy. Let us be of good cheer; Christ has borne the load before us, and the blood-stained footsteps of the King of Glory may be seen along the road which we traverse at this hour. There is something sweeter yet—Jesus was tempted, but Jesus never sinned. Then, my soul, it is not needful for you to sin, for Jesus was a man, and if one man endured these temptations and sinned not, then in His power His members may also cease from sin.

December 6

*W*e will never sing *Gloria in Excelsis* except if we pray to God *De Profundis*; out of the depths we must cry, or we will never behold glory in the highest. Prayer should be perfumed with love, saturated with love: love for our fellow saints and love for Christ. A man prevails in prayer only as he believes. The Holy Spirit is the author of faith and strengthens it so that we pray believing God's promise. Oh, that this blessed combination of excellent graces, priceless and sweet as the spices of the merchant, might be fragrant within us because the Holy Spirit is in our hearts!

Most blessed Comforter, exert Your mighty power within us, helping our infirmities in prayer.

December 7

And I will deliver thee out of the hand of the wicked, and I will redeem thee out of the hand of the terrible.
—Jeremiah 15:21

*N*ote the glorious personality of the promise—"I will...I will." The Lord Jehovah himself interposes to deliver and redeem His people. He pledges Himself personally to rescue them. His own arm will do it that He may have the glory. Neither our strength nor our weakness is taken into the account, but the lone *I*, like the sun in the heavens, shines out resplendent in all-sufficiency. Why then do we calculate our forces and consult with flesh and blood to our grievous wounding? Peace, you unbelieving thoughts; be still, and know that the Lord reigns.

December 8

*B*e it ever in your remembrance, that to keep strictly in the path of your Savior's command is better than any outward form of religion and to hearken to His precept with an attentive ear is better than to bring the fat of rams or any other precious thing to lay upon His altar. If you are failing to keep the least of Christ's commands to His disciples, I pray that you will be disobedient no longer. "To obey," even in the slightest and smallest thing, "is better than sacrifice" (1 Sam. 15:22). It is a blessed thing to be teachable as a little child, but it is a much more blessed thing when one has been taught the lesson to carry it out to the letter.

December 9

Our good Shepherd has in His flock a variety of experiences. Some are strong in the Lord, and others are weak in faith, but He is impartial in His care for all His sheep. The weakest lamb is as dear to Him as the most advanced in the flock. Lambs are accustomed to lag behind, prone to wander, and apt to grow weary, but from all the danger of these infirmities, the Shepherd protects them with His arm of power. He finds newborn souls, like your lambs, ready to perish; He nourishes them until life becomes vigorous. He finds weak minds ready to faint and die; He consoles them and renews their strength.

December 10

There are times in our spiritual experience when human counsel, sympathy, or religious ordinances fail to comfort or help us. Why does our gracious God permit this? Perhaps it is because we have been living too much without Him, and He therefore takes away everything upon which we have been in the habit of depending that He may drive us to Himself. It is a blessed thing to live at the fountainhead, having nothing of our own to trust to but resting upon the merits of Jesus. Beloved, when we are brought to a thirsting condition, we are sure to turn to the Fountain of Life with eagerness.

December 11

*I*t was a divine song which Habakkuk sang when in the night he said,

> *Although the fig tree shall not blossom, neither shall fruit be in the vines; the labour of the olive shall fail, and the fields shall yield no meat; the flock shall be cut off from the fold, and there shall be no herd in the stalls: Yet I will rejoice in the LORD, I will joy in the God of my salvation.*
> *(Hab. 3:17–18)*

No man can make a song in the night of himself. He may attempt it, but he will find that a song in the night must be divinely inspired. Oh, Chief Musician, let us not remain without song because affliction is upon us; tune our lips to the melody of thanksgiving.

December 12

*T*here are times when all the promises and doctrines of the Bible are of no avail unless a gracious hand will apply them to us. To meet this need there is one, the Spirit of Truth, who takes of the things of Jesus and applies them to us. Do not think that Christ has placed His joys on heavenly shelves that we may climb up to them for ourselves, but He draws near and sheds His peace in our hearts. Christian, if you are laboring today under deep distresses, your Father does not give you promises and then leave you to draw them from the Word, but the promises He has written in the Word He will write anew on your heart.

December 13

*G*od says to you, "Fear not...I am thy shield, and thy exceeding great reward" (Gen. 15:1). Believer, grasp the divine word with a personal, appropriating faith. Think that you hear Jesus say, "I have prayed for thee, that thy faith fail not" (Luke 22:32). Think you see Him walking on the waters of your trouble, for He is there, and He is saying, "Be of good cheer, it is I; be not afraid" (Matt. 14:27). Oh, those sweet words of Christ! May the Holy Spirit make you feel them as spoken to you. Forget the others for awhile—accept the voice of Jesus as addressed to you and say, "Jesus whispers consolation; I cannot refuse it; I will sit under His shadow with great delight."

December 14

*W*hen is the Christian most liable to sleep? Is it not when his temporal circumstances are prosperous? Have you not found it so? When you had daily troubles to take to the throne of grace, were you not more wakeful than you are now? Another dangerous time is when all goes pleasantly in spiritual matters. There is no temptation half so dangerous as not being tempted. The distressed soul does not sleep; it is after we enter into peaceful confidence and full assurance that we are in danger of slumbering. The disciples fell asleep after they had seen Jesus transfigured on the mountaintop. Take heed, joyous Christian; be as happy as you will, only be watchful.

*T*o give to others is but sowing seed for ourselves. He who is so good a steward as to be willing to use his substance for his Lord will be entrusted with more. Friend of Jesus, are you rendering Him according to the benefit received? Much has been given you—what is your fruit? Have you done all? Can you not do more? To be selfish is to be wicked. God forbid that any of us should follow the ungenerous and destructive policy of living for ourselves. Jesus pleased not Himself. All fullness dwells in Him, but "of his fulness have all we received" (John 1:16). Oh, for Jesus' spirit, that henceforth we may live not for ourselves!

December 16

But their eyes were holden that they should not know him.
—Luke 24:16

*T*he disciples had heard His voice so often and gazed upon that marred face so frequently that it is wonderful they did not discover Him. Yet is it not so with you also? You have not seen Jesus lately. You have been to His table, and you have not met Him there. You are in a dark trouble this day, and though He plainly says, "It is I; be not afraid" (Matt. 14:27), you cannot discern Him. Dear child of God, are you in this state? Faith alone can bring us to see Jesus. Make the following your prayer: "Lord, open my eyes that I may see my Savior present with me."

December 17

Our Lord would have all His people rich in high and happy thoughts concerning His blessed person. As a help to high thoughts of Christ, remember the estimation that Christ has beyond the skies. Think how God esteems the Only Begotten, His unspeakable gift to us. Consider what the angels think of Him as they count it their highest honor to veil their faces at His feet. Think of the mighty love which drew Him from His throne to die upon the cross! See Him risen, crowned, glorified! Bow before Him as the Wonderful, the Counselor, the mighty God, for only thus will your love to Him be what it should.

December 18

Oh, Christian, do you doubt as to whether God will fulfill His promise? Will the munitions of rock be carried by storm? Will the storehouses of heaven fail? Do you think that your heavenly Father, though He knows that you have need of food and clothing, will yet forget you? When not a sparrow falls to the ground without your Father knowing, and the very hairs of your head are all numbered (Matt. 10:29–30), will you mistrust and doubt Him? Full many there are who have been tried until at last they have been driven to exercise faith in God, and the moment of their faith has been the instant of their deliverance.

December 19

*A*re you willing, dear reader, to receive Christ? Then there is no difficulty in the way. Christ will be your guest; His own power is working with you, making you willing. What an honor to entertain the Son of God! The heaven of heavens cannot contain Him, and yet He condescends to find a house within our hearts! We are not worthy that He should come under our roof, but what an unutterable privilege when He condescends to enter! For then He makes a feast and causes us to feast with Him upon royal dainties. We sit at a banquet where He gives immortality to those who feed thereon. Blessed among the sons of Adam is he who entertains the Lord.

December 20

*I*n order to learn how to discharge your duty as a witness for Christ, look at His example. He is always witnessing: by the well of Samaria or in the temple of Jerusalem, by the lake of Gennesaret or on the mountain's brow. He witnesses so clearly and distinctly that there is no mistake in Him. Christian, make your life a clear testimony. Be as the brook wherein you may see every stone at the bottom. You need not say, "I am true"; be true. Study your great Exemplar, and be filled with His Spirit. Remember that you need much teaching, much upholding, much grace, and much humility if your witnessing is to be to your Master's glory.

December 21

*T*he more you know about Christ, the less will you be satisfied with superficial views of Him, and the more deeply you study His life and the fullness of His grace which shines in all His offices, the more truly will you see the King in His beauty. Long more and more to see Jesus. Meditation and contemplation are often like windows of agate and gates of carbuncle through which we behold the Redeemer. Meditation puts the telescope to the eye and enables us to see Jesus better than we could have seen Him if we had lived in the days of His flesh. Would that we were more taken up with the person, the work, and the beauty of our incarnate Lord.

December 22

*I*t is our wisdom, as well as our necessity, to beseech God continually to strengthen that which He has wrought in us. We often forget that the Author of our faith must be the Preserver of it also. The lamp which was burning in the temple was never allowed to go out, but it had to be daily replenished with fresh oil. In like manner, our faith can only live by being sustained with the oil of grace, and we can only obtain this from God Himself.

Let us, then, day by day, go to our Lord for the grace and strength we need. We have a strong argument to plead, for it is His own work of grace which we ask Him to strengthen. Only let your faith take hold of His strength.

December 23

*T*he distinguishing mark of a Christian is his confidence in the love of Christ and the yielding of his affections to Christ in return. First, faith sets her seal upon the man by enabling the soul to say with the apostle, "[Christ] loved me, and gave himself for me" (Gal. 2:20). Then love gives the countersign and stamps upon the heart gratitude and love to Jesus in return. "We love him, because he first loved us" (1 John 4:19). In those grand old ages, which are the heroic period of the Christian religion, this double mark was clearly to be seen in all believers in Jesus. They were men who knew the love of Christ and rested upon it as a man leans upon a staff whose trustiness he has tried.

December 24

*O*ur heavenly Father often draws us with the cords of love. How slowly do we respond to His gentle impulse! He draws us to exercise a more simple faith in Him, but we have not yet attained to Abraham's confidence. We do not leave our worldly cares with God. Our meager faith brings leanness into our souls. We do not open our hearts wide, though God has promised to fill them. Does He not this day draw us to trust Him? Can we not hear Him say, "Come, My child, and trust Me. The veil is rent; enter into My presence. I am worthy of your fullest confidence; cast your cares on Me. Shake yourself from the dust of your cares, and put on your beautiful garments of joy."

December 25

We esteem every day alike, but still, as the season suggests thoughts of Jesus, let us joyfully remember our dear Redeemer's glorious birth. Who but He was ever longed for by such a multitude of hearts? When did angels indulge in midnight songs or did God hang a new star in the sky? To whose cradle did rich and poor make so willing a pilgrimage and offer such hearty and unsought offerings? Well may earth rejoice; well may all men cease their labor to celebrate "the great birthday" of Jesus. Let gladness rule the hour; let holy song and sweet heart music accompany our soul in the raptures of joy.

December 26

What bliss to be a perfectly pardoned soul! My soul dedicates all her powers to Him who, of His own unpurchased love, became my surety and wrought out for me redemption through His blood! What riches of grace does free forgiveness exhibit! To forgive at all, to forgive fully, to forgive freely, to forgive ever! Here is a constellation of wonders, and when I think of how great my sins were, how dear were the precious drops which cleansed me from them, I am in a maze of wondering, worshipping affection. I bow before the throne which absolves me; I clasp the cross which delivers me; I serve henceforth the Incarnate God through whom I am this day a pardoned soul.

*A*t this hour we rest in the promises of our faithful God, knowing that His words are full of truth and power. We rest in the doctrines of His Word, which are consolation itself. We rest in the covenant of His grace, which is a haven of delight. The person of Jesus is the quiet resting place of His people, and when we draw near to Him in the breaking of bread, in the hearing of the Word, in the searching of the Scriptures, in prayer, or in praise, we find any form of approach to Him to be the return of peace to our spirits. The God of Peace gives perfect peace to those whose hearts are stayed upon Him.

December 28

*N*othing can satisfy the entire man but the Lord's love and the Lord's own self. To embrace our Lord Jesus, to dwell in His love, and to be fully assured of union with Him—this is all in all. Dear reader, you need not try other forms of life in order to see whether they are better than the Christian's. If you roam the world around, you will see no sights like the sight of the Savior's face. If you could have all the comforts of life but lost your Savior, you would be wretched; however, if you win Christ, you would find it a paradise. Should you live in obscurity or die with famine, you will yet be satisfied with favor and be full of the goodness of the Lord.

December 29

*H*is presence will be realized most by those who are most like Him. If you desire to see Christ, you must grow in conformity to Him. Bring yourself, by the power of the Spirit, into union with Christ's desires and motives and plans of action, and you will be in fellowship with Him. Remember His presence may be had, and His promise is as true as ever. He delights to be with us. If He does not come, it is because we hinder Him by our indifference. He will reveal Himself to our earnest prayers and graciously suffer himself to be detained by our entreaties and by our tears, for these are the golden chains which bind Jesus to His people.

December 30

*C*hrist appears as a shepherd to His own sheep, not to others. As soon as He appears, His own sheep perceive Him. They trust Him, and they are prepared to follow Him. He knows them, and they know Him. There is a mutual knowledge and a constant connection between them. Thus the one mark, the sure mark, the infallible mark of regeneration and adoption is a hearty faith in the appointed Redeemer. Reader, are you in doubt, are you uncertain whether you bear the secret mark of God's children? Then let not an hour pass over your head until you have said, "Search me, O God, and know my heart" (Ps. 139:23).

*I*n the last day, that great day of the feast, Jesus stood and cried, saying, If any man thirst, let him come unto me, *and* drink" (John 7:37). No other distinction is made but that of thirst. No waiting or preparation is so much as hinted at. Drinking represents a reception for which no fitness is required. Sinful lips may touch the stream of divine love; they cannot pollute it but will themselves be purified. Jesus is the fount of hope. Dear reader, hear the dear Redeemer's loving voice as He cries to each of us, "If any man thirst, let him come unto me, and drink."